W9-CHO-828

BREATHING
UNDERWATER

A Caregiver's Journey of Hope

Eileen Benthal

Free Indeed
Freelance Service

When the Son sets you free, you are free indeed. (John 8:36)

ACKNOWLEDGMENTS

Thanks to my fellow warrior Mom and gifted writer, Jeannie Ewing. Your prayerful perspective and your excellent grammar really helped make this possible. To Andrea Bontempi, your detailed editing skills made this book tight and more readable. Thanks to Jeannie & Bill Husing for sharing the cottages at the beach to write and pray! To my son, David thank you for your outstanding photography work on the cover. Glad the Peconic Bay was warm the first week of October! Thanks also to my sister-in-law, Carol Benthal-Bingley for your diligence and creativity in the graphic design of the book.

Finally, thank you to my dear husband, Steve for always stepping up to the plate to learn whatever new skills we need to get the job done! Thank you for your endless hours, your patience and your love. You are the wind beneath my wings, always believing that I can fly.

Thank you all!

I thank my God upon every remembrance of you.
Philippians 1:3

THE REASON FOR MY HOPE

God spoke to me in my eighth grade class in the public school. I guess He didn't get the memo that prayer was not allowed.

I was an upperclassman in the middle school where I survived and actually made some great friends. It was my last year before high school, and I was more than a little nervous. But when I took my seat near the window and glanced up at the poster on the bulletin board, I knew I was home in this classroom.

Right there, in my eighth grade class, God spoke to me through a pretty poster of a sunrise on the water that read:

> *Let your light shine before others, that they may see your good deeds and glorify your Father in heaven.*   Matthew 5:16

God had been speaking to me a lot about light. My name, Eileen, in Gaelic means "Light." My maiden name is Devine. I was most certainly prepared to let my light, who I am in name and person, shine before others even as early as the eighth grade. Ever since I could remember, my mother told me that she knew I was special from my birth. I was the only one of her eight children whom she did not see born. The umbilical cord had wrapped around my neck, and the doctors knocked her out so that they could save my life. When she finally saw me the next day, she said that she knew God had saved me for a very special purpose. I am eternally grateful to my mother for the encouragement she gave by believing in me and that God had a special plan for my life. This deep sense of purpose is the conviction that defines my life.

I was raised in an Irish Catholic family where faith and folklore were woven into daily life just like Irish trinkets and the rosary beads that lay side by side on my grandmother Nanny's bedside table. I was so impressed by Nanny's faith. The way she sat by her husband's side every day at the convalescent home, her dancing blue eyes and soft aging skin radiated with an aged devotion that testified to her belief in the Sacrament of Holy Matrimony. Her kitchen, very clean and white, smelled pure and holy, right up to the Statue of the Blessed Virgin Mary that looked down on us from the top of the refrigerator. Though the room was chilly, because the steam heat couldn't keep up with the drafty windows of her Connecticut home, the kitchen was always warmed by the smell of tea brewing. I never knew that tea could be served black—only cream and sugar at Nanny's house.

I remember walking Nanny back to her home from a family party at my aunt's house. When we got into her house, we walked passed the portraits of President Kennedy and his family hanging on the wall next to the Irish blessing. Nanny let down her long silver hair and brushed it gently before she put on her nightgown and got ready for bed. I sat and listened to her goodnight prayers to the Lord and His Mother as Nanny asked them to watch over the entire family, her children, grandchildren and all those she had promised to pray for. I chuckled as she whispered in her Irish brogue, "And Sweet Jesus, Mary and Joseph, please wake me up if anything should go wrong in this house as I sleep. We will take care of it together." My Nanny inspired me with the faith of the Ancients.

Inspired by Nanny's witness and my mother's promise of a purpose-filled life, I decided to walk with Christ, literally. At my First Communion, Fr. O'Brien told us that Jesus was calling us to walk with

Him every day. Being the literal eight year old that I was, I listened intently as I imagined ways that I could walk with Jesus—even though I couldn't see Him.

The very next morning, I awoke anxious to keep my promise and to begin this new life with Jesus. I got dressed and ran outside and asked Jesus if He was ready to go for our first walk. As I walked around the block, I extended my left hand and imagined that Jesus was holding it as we moved at a steady pace. I imagined this handsome and smiling Jesus, walking along beside me, laughing with me as we chatted about life, my family and my First Communion. This was the beginning of my walk with Jesus. Although I dropped my hand at times and diverged slightly from the path, He never left my side.

One would think that a decision made at such a young age would seal one's life for sanctity. I, however, traversed through my teenage years experiencing some of the same struggles most young people do. I dabbled in some risky behaviors that involved experimenting slightly with alcohol and intense dating relationships where I gave my heart too quickly. But that sense of God's presence never left me. I had an intimate knowledge of God's love and always a profound sense of my call to go deeper with God.

At my Confirmation, I was introduced to another role model of faith: Saint Elizabeth Ann Seton. St. Elizabeth was the first native born American to be canonized. She was canonized in 1975—just four years before I was confirmed. She lived during the Revolutionary War period—my favorite time in history. She was raised in a Protestant home and had a profound love for the Bible. She married the love of her life and led him to Christ, and the two remained faithful in the midst of extreme economic struggles and life threatening illnesses. After her husband died, St. Elizabeth realized she longed for deeper intimacy with Jesus in the Eucharist and the maternal love of His Mother, Mary. It was her search of greater fulfillment that brought her to the Catholic Church. She converted to Catholicism, raised her children in the faith and went on to found a religious order, two orphanages and a school.

Mother Seton was everything I wanted to be: a wife, a mother and a saint. I wanted all of that and so I took Elizabeth as my confirmation name and pledged to follow in her footsteps in my adult commitment to Christ.

Even with my earthly and heavenly role models solidly leading me in faith, the tug of worldly desire and an intense need for peer approval caused me to dabble in the parties of youth. I thought I could live in both worlds and walk the fence between a Godly life and the satisfaction of those desires. Going to Saturday evening Mass fulfilled both. I would put in the time at Church and head to a Saturday evening party at a friend's house or at a bonfire in the woods near our church and school.

One such Saturday evening, I was particularly bold. After Mass, I approached the Tabernacle, the Holy of Holies for Catholics, where Jesus Himself reposes in the Blessed Sacrament. I spoke to my friend, Jesus. I said, "Dearest Jesus, I am sorry for the party that I am going to tonight. Please help me to make better decisions and when I fall, please be there to forgive me tomorrow. Amen."

Now, as an adult, I marvel and shudder at my childish presumption before the Almighty God. Still, nothing quite prepared me for the next moments as I knelt before that Tabernacle. I heard a voice in my head say to me, "I want to make an example of your life. If you follow Me, I will lead you to witness to thousands of people throughout your life. I will use you to draw them to me."

Yikes. I remember looking intently at the Tabernacle in disbelief, saying "Amen" as I made the Sign of the Cross and went on my way. I know I went to the party that night. I don't recall what happened, but

I do recall that my teenage years began to clearly turn towards the Lord after hearing that reply from God.

Despite my strong foundation in faith, or maybe because I had this early taste of heaven, I struggled with depression in my adolescent and teenage years. As I look back now on that time through the lens of wisdom, I realize that spiritual warfare, emotional trauma and hormonal imbalances played heavily into this struggle. Nonetheless, I was sometimes taunted with thoughts of suicide during those teenage years.

After a difficult tonsillectomy that caused profuse internal bleeding, I came up with a plan. It was in the moments just before the execution of the plan, as I stood with a life-threatening overdose in my hands, that I looked in the mirror and faced the pain of trying to live a holy life on my own strength. Weary from the battle of youth, and with the eternal hope of heaven before me, I dropped the pills into the bathroom sink and once again cried out to God.

I said, "Lord, I can't do this by myself anymore. Please help me to live my life for You and with You." In that moment, I imagined a chorus of angels singing as all of heaven rejoiced and I heard these words, "Hallelujah! You don't have to do it by yourself anymore. I Am with you always!"

Around that same time, my father introduced me to the Catholic Charismatic Renewal, a profound movement of the power of the Holy Spirit within the Catholic Church. In the Charismatic Renewal, I learned about the gifts of the Holy Spirit and experienced worshiping God in spontaneous and heartfelt song and petitions filled with praise. It was a transforming experience of God for me, an expression of faith that seemed to pour from my heart. I learned to hear God's voice more clearly. The Scriptures came alive as God's personal word to me and the teachings of the Catholic Church resounded as truth in my heart.

I began keeping a journal for creative writing and for prayer, and I discovered an intense desire to pray for the needs of others.

My parents and I frequented a few prayer meetings every month, each characterized by spontaneous expressions of praise, sharing of personal testimony and melodic songs that led our hearts and minds to focus on Jesus.

At one such prayer meeting, I had yet another profound experience of God that refined my call to live a life of faith and purpose. During a time of spontaneous worship, I had my eyes closed and I saw this vision: I was standing out in the middle of white light. Jesus was walking towards me, His Mother at His side. She placed a full blossomed rose, without a stem, into my cupped hands. Jesus gently held my hands in His as He instructed me to lift them up toward heaven. As I lifted my hands, the rose began to beam with bright yellow streams of light emanating from its petals, through my hands and penetrating out into the white light surrounding us. At that moment, the leader of the prayer meeting shared a word for the group as he said, "This little rose has become a light to the nations." My eyes startled open as I looked around wondering if he also saw the vision I had just seen in my imagination. But as the prayer meeting continued, I realized that the Spirit was confirming the vision and giving me a word outside of myself just so I would believe.

At that point, finally, there was no turning back. Not that I was perfect or that anything about my life would characterize me as holier than any other teenager transitioning to young adulthood, but I could no longer negate the words, the visions, and the hope of this call that God had placed on my life since my creation in my mother's womb. Forging ahead to pursue this call to sanctity and this mission of purpose, I chose a career path of ministry in the Catholic Church. I went on to study theology and attend Franciscan University in Steubenville, Ohio.

Franciscan University is a small Catholic college nestled like a light on the cliffs of the Ohio River. The University wed my two loves: a vibrant personal relationship with Jesus in the context of the traditions of the Catholic Faith. At Franciscan, I could be immersed in my faith and learn to live a holy and healthy life. At one of the very first liturgies that I attended as a student there, I poured out my sorrow to the Lord for a lifetime of sin. I felt as though I sat in the pew in Christ the King Chapel with a covering of rags, wondering how God could forgive me for my insolent behaviors in the face of His great Mercy.

At that Mass, the God of heaven and earth came to me in the form of bread and wine and spoke gently to my broken heart. He promised me that while even now, I felt clothed in rags of sin and unworthy of His Love, He would make all things new. God called me His Beloved as He promised me, "In these next four years, I shall take from you these rags and the sin that clings to you. We shall write our love story as you learn to pray and live this spousal relationship with me. As you came here in rags, you will leave this place dressed as a bride, knowing that I am indeed your Bridegroom and you are my bride." I went to Confession that evening and laid my tattered rags at the Lord's feet ready to begin this new life, learning to live as Jesus' bride.

Four years later, I literally left Franciscan dressed as a Bride, only after walking down the aisle of Christ the King Chapel to be joined to the love of my life, my husband, Steve, to begin our new life together. In those four years I grew in body, mind and spirit and sought to embrace St. Paul's instruction.

Do not be conformed to the pattern of this world, but be transformed by the renewal of your minds, that you may judge what is God's will, what is good, pleasing and perfect.
Romans 12:2

There is no greater witness of Christ and His love for His Church than the union of a man and a woman in marriage. It is no wonder why today such confusion stirs over the definition of marriage as God's message of love through the intimate union of man and woman. In our faithful commitment and indeed in our brokenness, my husband and I stand as a witness to God's unfailing love for His Beloved. And from this union, we became co-creators of miracles. Together we gave life to eight children, four living and four in heaven. In everyday life, we have witnessed the wonders God has done.

This book recounts my journey as a woman, a mother and as a caregiver to my youngest daughter. Johanna was born with CCM3, a rare genetic and neurological disease that causes malformations in the brain to multiply and hemorrhage. In eighteen years, Johanna has had over 90 surgeries and most of those have been in her brain.

I have a special place in my heart for caregivers because I am one. Family caregivers are a special group of people whose love for family members requires great sacrifices of time, energy and resources. The hours are endless, and it can be said that we often feel as though we are drowning in our circumstances. I have written this book especially for you.

I am frequently asked, "How do you do it?" Supposing that "it" refers to living life to the fullest while caring for my precious daughter whose needs are chronic and can quickly become emergent, I must share from a faith perspective. My faith imbues everything I do. To share strategies for caregivers without sharing my faith would be for me akin to offering someone a ride to reach their destination without putting gas in the car. My faith is the power on this journey of hope.

In the first three chapters, I share with you the miracles that laid the foundation and defined this journey. Eighteen years ago, I had a nightmare that I quickly realized was a warning of the difficulties we would encounter. As the nightmares continued, so did the trials of life. Years later, the voice of God transformed my nightmare into a dream which offered me a future of hope. In the following seven chapters, I present my strategy for hope using the acronym: *B-R-E-A-T-H-E*. More than "how to" advice, these chapters offer you, the reader, an invitation and a challenge to change your perspective on the trials you are experiencing in your life.

I love this quote from Former First Lady Rosalyn Carter: "There are only four kinds of people in this world—those who have been caregivers, those who currently are caregivers, those who will be caregivers and those who need caregivers."

All of us can relate to care-giving in one way or another. Each of us needs to care: for ourselves, for those we love and for the world around us. If you are reading this book, you too may feel like you are drowning in your hopeless situations and difficult circumstances. It is my prayer that, in this story, you may experience hope for your own journey and the power to breathe underwater.

In Hope,

Eileen Benthal

CHAPTER ONE

THE NIGHTMARE

The ocean water was black and cold against the grey skies. There appeared no light in the horizon or overhead. No stars, no sun, and no direction, only me treading water in this vast ocean with my newborn baby in my arms, desperately struggling to keep us from drowning. We were alone in the middle of the dark ocean.

Suddenly I woke up drenched with sweat and leaking milk. It was the hot end of August and though my skin stuck to the sheets, on the inside I felt cold like death. I took a deep breath as I opened my eyes to see my newborn baby girl safely cradled in my arms. I kissed her sweet little head and studied her tiny features as she slept peacefully next to me in our king size bed. I told myself that it was only a nightmare, this reoccurring sight that woke me numerous times since Johanna was born. I had never experienced post-partum depression after the birth of my three older children. But everything about this baby and this experience was different. I knew it in my bones.

When she stirred, she opened her tiny mouth and her head moved back and forth until at last she could latch on to nurse. I felt relief as the milk let down and began to flow into Johanna's mouth. The cold and powerless feeling of the nightmare ebbed into my subconscious, replaced by warmth and a deep sense of security as my body and soul nourished my baby at the breast.

The nightmares happened just about every night, and the uneasy feeling was always with me, right from the beginning. It began in the labor and delivery room when I first held Johanna in my arms.

Johanna was our fourth baby. We had three older children: our son was nine and two other daughters were six and three. I nursed them all into toddlerhood, La Leche League style, wearing them in a sling during the day and sleeping with them by my side at night. Despite concerns raised by our parents, my husband Steve and I were perfectly content to have our kids around. We were a close-knit family and were very excited about our latest addition. As excited as we were, there was a strange apprehension that I experienced with Johanna. These nightmares were also reminiscent of one I had when my son was born.

My son's birth was eventful for a first-born. My water broke with no signs of active labor, and despite my preparations, he arrived via C-section in a sterile operating room as I lay on the table. As the surgeon struggled to stop the bleeding, the nurses whisked my husband and son out of the operating room. With his son in his arms, my husband heard one of the nurses say that the doctor had better control the bleeding before I died on the table. My husband did the only he could do; he prayed and rocked our son, David, hoping that he would not become a father and a widower all in a day.

Thankfully, after they stopped the bleeding and gave me a transfusion, I was finally able to hold David for the first time. Elated feelings of motherhood pushed away all the concerns of the delivery as we settled in for a weekend of recovery in the hospital. Then, on the following Monday, just three days after David was born, I had my very first post-partum nightmare.

In the dream, I was an invisible outsider watching as my family mourned the loss of someone they loved. I remember feeling like it was a scene from "A Christmas Carol," and I wondered if perhaps I had hemorrhaged to death after all. I saw my brother comforting my family members and specifically going to my parents' home to tell them someone had died.

When I woke up the next morning to my son's cries, I forgot about the nightmare. My husband came to the hospital and had everything ready for me to leave. The doctor said we were ready to be released. We packed everything up, baby in tow and headed home. Then, on our way home, a car ran through an intersection and nearly hit us. My husband slammed on the brakes just in time. I quickly checked on our baby who was secure and sleeping in his car seat in the back of the car. When my husband slammed on the brakes, I had a sudden flash of that nightmare from the night before. It was now vivid in my mind. I explained it to my husband as he drove the rest of the way home. He was oddly quiet; I attributed it to the exhausting excitement of being new parents.

When we got home, I was tucked into bed with the baby. We set everything within reach so that I didn't have to get out of bed to lift David out of the bassinet to nurse and change his diaper.

After we were settled in, my husband paused to tell me he had something important to share with me. I could tell by the look on his face that it was very bad news. With tears in his eyes he recounted a tragic story of my older sister's death. She was struck head on by a drunk driver and was dead at the scene of the crash. My nephew, eleven at the time, was spared. My sister had pushed him under the dashboard of the passenger side of their car and out of the way of the oncoming car.

I was very upset at this, but I immediately realized that the dream I had the night before served as a warning. It was a miraculous preparation to ease some of the shock of this news. I later learned that it was indeed my older brother who had conveyed the tragic news to our parents that night. My sister died in the early evening of that same night. It was as if I was transported to be with my grieving parents, even as I slept with my newborn son.

That first night at home, I woke up to nurse my son. It was at that time that I turned my thoughts to prayer. I whispered thanks to God for the blessings of this beautiful baby in my arms as the tears rolled down my cheeks and reached his tiny cheeks nursing at my breast. God spoke to me in the depths of my heart and said, "In case you forgot that I give new life in the midst of death, I gave you David as a reminder of this truth. I give new life in the midst of death. Have faith and you will see."

Because of the severity of the hemorrhage during the C-section and the need for a blood transfusion, I did not make the trip to Connecticut from Long Island to attend my sister's wake and funeral. My husband and I were caretakers living in a retreat house at the time. So we were able to plan our own memorial Mass with friends.

The Mass was intimate and honoring of my sister's memory and our new miracle. During the homily, the Priest asked me to share about my sister. I shared a little about Kathy's life, her dedication to motherhood and to teaching children. She was the first of my seven siblings to marry and the first one to have children.

When I was ten years old I became an aunt. I learned from my sister how to mother children from instinct and love. She also nursed her two kids, despite criticisms from family and friends. I spent a lot of time with her family as a mother's helper. We camped together by the beaches in Connecticut and Rhode Island. Kathy was my first role model for mothering, and I so appreciated her for those memories.

At this memorial, I shared with our friends about the nightmare which became a gentle warning to prepare my soul for grief. Finally, I introduced our newborn son, David, as the sign of hope that indeed the Lord brings life in the midst of death.

Almost ten years and three children later, I found myself wondering if this ocean nightmare was also some kind of message. While I enjoyed my baby Johanna, there was a nagging feeling inside that something was not right. Each day I prayed and pondered. I kept sensing that God was telling me to trust my instincts—that I was a very good mother who knew what her children needed.

When Johanna went for one of her first newborn check-ups, I shared my concerns with our pediatrician. She was a little concerned with the way Johanna preferred to tilt her head to the right and seemed to have some difficulty following my voice. It was almost as if she had a stiff neck. But then again, newborns are just developing muscle tone and it's difficult to discern a problem. Still, being cautiously optimistic, the doctor sent us to a neurologist for further testing.

The day of Johanna's first neurology exam, she was completely fine. She made eye contact and cooed. She even seemed to turn her head toward me. The doctor did notice some resistance at turning her head and diagnosed her with a stiff neck as he wrote a script for physical therapy. I told the neurologist about a disturbing few moments I experienced when I was burping Johanna on my lap. As I rolled her over, she had a weird smile and her lips were purple. I cried out for help, but in that instant, her color returned and she was totally appropriate again.

The neurologist didn't think much of it except to say that there was a small possibility that it was a brief seizure. Then, the doctor looked me in the eye and said that what he had the most faith in was mother's intuition.

He asked me directly, "You are the mother of four children. You've done this before. What do you think of this baby?" With tears in my eyes I said, "Doctor, I believe that there is something terribly wrong with this baby, something that we can't yet see." He replied, "Well then, we are going to keep a careful eye on her."

He went on to order some testing for seizures at a later date and called the pediatrician to share those concerns. All the doctors rallied, measuring Johanna's head, watching for any indication of neurological problems or otherwise. I felt extremely supported by them. I hoped that if the time came that Johanna needed more help, we would all know what to do.

The time came soon, one morning during daily Mass, just after I received Communion. Johanna was in the baby sling sleeping and I was running my hand over the top of her tiny head as I had done so many times before. My hand stopped in the middle of her head. Where her soft spot usually felt indented, it was now raised and filled with a palpable fluid. I darted out after Mass and went home to call the doctor. When the physician's assistant called me back, I explained what I felt and that today happened to be the day we were scheduled for the seizure monitoring. She told me to go to that appointment, ask the neurologist what he thought, and then call back.

As I was getting ready, my son said, "Mom, I've been reading the baby development charts and Johanna is not doing those things they say three month old babies do. Can you tell the doctor?" I hugged him and told him that I was heading to the doctor's office and would tell him everything.

My three older kids kissed Johanna and me goodbye as I headed out the door. Little did we all know that this was the last time they would see their baby sister at home for weeks. Our lives would never be the same again.

That was the beginning of a long day of evaluations and consultations that led us to the emergency room where a neurologist told my husband and me that our baby had hydrocephalus, a build-up of fluid compressing her brain. They told us that it was an emergency situation which would require brain surgery that evening to drain the fluid and keep her safe. But first they needed to do a CT scan of her brain.

I asked, "Will a CT scan show a brain tumor?" Surprised by my question, the doctor responded, "It will, if there is one." My husband was equally surprised by my question.

I will never forget the long, dark hallway where my husband and I waited while Johanna was having her first brain scan. The two of us were silent, though our glistening eyes met often. When the doctor emerged from the reading area, he asked us to come inside to view the scan. I still remember what that scan looked like that dreadful night. Johanna's brain was covered in large pools of fluid.

It looked like her brain was drowning in an ocean.

My mind immediately recalled that vast dark ocean of my nightmares, and it all made sense. Rather than feeling overwhelmed and devastated by the news, I felt relieved.

I found myself whispering thanks to God for so great a mercy. Once again, I was subconsciously prepared for this journey and given all I needed intuitively to keep my baby safe. Because of this foreboding nightmare, I pursued medical advice. Otherwise evaluations that would have been scheduled appointments could have happened too late. Because of inspired intuition, I noticed details about my newborn daughter, even from the delivery room, that might have gone unchecked.

I followed my heart, and now Johanna was safe getting the medical care she so desperately needed. I finally knew that I wasn't losing my mind down the slippery slope of postpartum hormones. Rather, I was supernaturally inspired, my intuition heightened by a profound grace of God to sustain us through the trial ahead. I felt tremendous relief as a heavy knowledge and burden that I had been bearing on my own was now shared by others who could help save Johanna's life.

The doctor was a young resident covering the night shift. He searched our faces as he explained that the fluid compressing Johanna's brain was extremely dangerous and needed to be drained immediately. It was already 10 p.m.

My husband couldn't speak and looked as if he would die of a broken heart. I asked questions to understand the situation better, and within a short amount of time, I grasped both the severity and the anatomy of this life threatening situation. It seemed that there was a large mass on our baby's brain that was blocking the flow of the cerebral spinal fluid (CSF). This fluid cushions the brain and washes over it, and is found in small pockets called ventricles.

Normal ventricles look like small ponds, set nicely in the brain. In Johanna's case, these ventricles were drastically expanded because of the blockage, and now they literally looked like an ocean threatening to drown her brain in CSF.

That night, I discovered that I had a natural aptitude for understanding basics of human anatomy and neurology. While I had never been educated in biology or done any extensive study in human anatomy, I discovered the beginning of an innate sense that would serve Johanna and our family well for years to come.

I believe that the doctor was surprised and perplexed by my seemingly cool demeanor in the face of such devastating news. He probably thought that I was just in shock, and maybe I was in some sort of shocked state. However, I felt relieved knowing and facing the difficult situation before us rather than dealing with a gnawing sense of impending doom that left me feeling powerless and alone.

When they wheeled Johanna out in the stretcher, both my husband and I saw the effects of this condition causing a steep decline. Whereas the signs and symptoms had been gradual and slow, now they appeared to be progressing faster. The fluid bulged from the opening in her skull and her eyes were heavy from the pressure in her brain, causing a life threatening condition referred to as "sun setting ." We were going to lose her that night unless she got into the operating room for brain surgery. As they rushed us to the Pediatric Intensive Care Unit (PICU), the doctor and my husband walked in silence. I needed to talk so I started the conversation.

"This might sound crazy, but I feel relieved," I began. "I knew that there was something seriously wrong with my baby. Somehow, I believe that God was preparing me for this."

The doctor's head hung low as he shook it and said, "No one can ever be prepared for something like this."

My husband looked into my eyes, seemingly longing to feel some of the consolation I felt but at a profound loss for words. He admired my connection to God and the consolation that faith brought me, but in that moment, it was eclipsed by grief. We rode the elevator in silence, gathering strength for the long night ahead.

As the doors swung open to the Pediatric Intensive Care Unit (PICU), we were ushered into a sea of faces. Doctors, nurses and other support staff were all there to see Johanna and get her assessed and into the operating room as soon as possible.

The PICU doctors expressed their concern and asked to examine our baby girl before speaking to us. The nurse asked us to leave the room for a moment so that they could put in an IV and take report from the neurology resident. The air was thick with tension, but there was also a sense of great confidence as the PICU staff attended to our daughter.

Then, someone asked if we could take a phone call, and immediately I remembered my other three children who were being cared for by Johanna's godparents. I got on the phone and explained that Johanna had a large tumor in her brain. My dear friend broke down and asked what the next step would be for Johanna as she assured me not to worry about our three older children. I thanked her as I said goodbye.

After that, we were ushered into a room with a neurologist and a neurosurgeon. They explained the severity of our daughter's condition and the need for emergency surgery to relieve the fluid pressure on her brain. They were going to put a drain in one of the ventricles in her brain, and the fluid would then be shunted to a tube positioned on the outside of her crib.

The operation was straightforward for them, life saving for our daughter, and a life altering decision that would affect the rest of our lives. We signed the first of many consent forms granting the doctors permission to operate. Then we went back into the room to be with our baby.

Johanna was barely recognizable with all the monitors and the IV, the very simplest devices she would have for quite some time. She did not respond to my voice. She was listless and sleepy from the pressure on her brain.

Soon her godfather joined us. He is a nurse by profession and the father of seven. He was a welcome sight in the sea of strange faces. He listened to the explanations, asked really good questions and then helped us to focus on our baby. The three of us gathered our strength as we prayed over Johanna, asking God to protect and heal our little one. As the doctors were rushing her to the operating room, they told us where to wait and gave us one last chance to kiss our baby—they stopped short of saying-goodbye. None of us knew what would happen. She was where she had been all along—in God's hands.

The surgical waiting room was filled with people, just a blur of faces, until we realized that we recognized a few of them. Some people from our church and our pastor came to support us. Bad news travels fast, which can be a good thing and a bad thing sometimes. For us it was a welcome distraction from the roller-coaster ride.

The first thing people asked was how Johanna was, and the next thing was what could be done. Johanna's godfather made some calls at the pay phone (this was before we carried cell phones, let alone smart phones). His wife took our younger children home to their own beds and stayed the night to care for them. Other friends arranged meals for the family and took our puppy (adopting a puppy was a postpartum decision that I had recently made under stress).

For the first time that crazy day, my husband and I embraced as our pastor prayed aloud over us. I remember that we cried with deeply pained sighs, and tears streamed down our cheeks. I also remember that the feeling of peace never left me. I felt fearful and confused, but more than anything else, I felt loved and supported.

In the back of my mind was the nightmare, but now I knew there was a reason, an answer to the nagging questions that plagued me for three months. As words of consolation and strength flowed from the priest, grace overflowed to all around us.

After what seemed like an eternity to us, the doctor emerged from the operating room to say that Johanna did well and we could see her again in the PICU. After she was transferred, we were allowed to see her. Now, in addition to the IV and the monitors, there was an arterial line monitoring blood pressure and a large and intricate drain flowing from her brain into a sterile sealed container on the outside of the crib.

For the first time in almost 24 hours, Johanna's eyes were clear when she awoke, and she seemed to recognize me and made eye contact. Still sleepy from the anesthesia, she drifted back to sleep as my husband prepared to leave and I settled in for the night.

This would be just the first of many nights that I would be separated from my husband and other children. Again, we wept and prayed as we kissed each other goodbye. I longed to go home with him and cuddle up with all my children. My breasts were full of milk but my baby was not yet able to nurse. My body was getting ready to take back its place in the care and provision for my baby.

I pulled up two hard chairs and stretched my legs with a blanket over me as I kept vigil at my daughter's side. A few hours later, my baby's cries caused my milk to let down as I was startled awake from my light slumber. The nurse came in with a bottle when I took my first step into advocacy for this baby. Hours ago she needed brain surgery. But now she needed me, and I was more than happy to help her.

At first, the nurses discouraged me from nursing, explaining that Johanna couldn't really change positions yet. The drain in her brain worked on gravity and it needed to remain at the level it was to keep it from draining too much or too little. Then, they said we could try to move her together, but Johanna cried and vomited when we changed positions. If this had been my first baby, nursing might have ended then and there, thus interrupting a vital physical and emotional bond that was as critical for Johanna as it was for me. But because she was my fourth baby and I was an educated and experienced nursing mom, I found a solution.

Every nursing mother knows that there is only one way to nurse your baby while the car is moving; you lean over the car seat. This little trick of the trade has scandalized more than a few passing cars (and delighted a few truck drivers). It served us well in the PICU predicament. The nurse helped me to lower one of the side rails of the crib as I leaned beside Johanna to nurse. The positioning was tricky and her suck was a little weak at first. But then, as both she and I settled in, the maternal bond took over to heal both our bodies and our emotions from the turmoil of the previous day.

Finally, I was able to do something for my baby girl that came so naturally to me. A few hours later, I laughed when I heard the doctors making rounds outside the door of the hospital room. We were in a state teaching hospital, so there were many medical students as well as attending physicians and specialists who needed to be included in my daughter's care.

They discussed her case as a group both to offer input and to provide education for the residents in training. In some ways, it offered us better care because there were more minds studying our daughter. On the other hand, sometimes I had to step in to ensure that her needs for sleep and comfort were cared for before more doctors tried to examine her for their reports.

That morning, I heard them discussing her case, specifically nutrition. They accurately reported that she was an exclusively breast fed baby. Then one of the residents commented, "Mom insists on nursing although it is difficult because of the positional nature of the ventricular drain in the baby's head." When asked how I was doing this, the doctor explained that I was leaning over the crib to nurse Johanna. Then another doctor asked, "Why?"—as if I was unaware that my baby could be fed by a bottle or by a tube for that matter. I had a million reasons why, beginning with "why not?"

The responses were hushed as I imagined them saying, "She's in the PICU. We have the technology, Mom doesn't need to nurse." Johanna needed me, and I needed Johanna to do something normal for both of us.

Following the doctor rounds, we were informed that Johanna would need an MRI which would take a careful look at the tumor in her brain, and then another neurosurgeon would come to speak with us to plan the next step. I couldn't think of the next step, only the one right in front of me. Now that the fluid was draining, Johanna's brain wasn't under pressure so our baby began to coo and laugh for the very first time. While the doctors planned the MRI, I started advocating for her siblings to visit.

It was a long day of testing and discussions. The general consensus was not a good one. We were told that the tumor on Johanna's brain appeared cancerous, and it was compressing her brainstem, the core of the brain that sustained respiratory functions. They said that while the tumor had to be removed, the possibility existed that as the brainstem bounced back into place, Johanna could stroke and die.

My husband and I got permission for our other kids to visit their sister, not wanting her to die before they could say goodbye. The pressure in her brain was being controlled so they could see her laugh and smile. Obviously they were deeply concerned—they missed her. My ten year-old David had the cutest reply to my husband's sharing about CT scans. He said; "If cats can see Johanna, why can't we?" Out of the mouths of babes comes the joy of innocence and a balm for the weary souls.

As I drifted off to sleep that night, I realized that since this ordeal started, I did not have one ocean nightmare. With Johanna carefully watched in the PICU, I could finally get some rest and take a breath without treading water.

CHAPTER TWO

PATH OF MIRACLES

As Johanna stabilized, plans were made for the resection of the brain-stem tumor. Rumors were flying in the hospital. My husband actually heard two residents in the elevator discussing the case of the poor little baby with a huge brain tumor, who would most likely die. That was before there was a sign reminding them not to discuss patients in the elevator and before patient privacy rights were respected and enforced.

Visitors came in droves. Friends and friends of friends came with offers of prayer and help. We didn't have any family on Long Island, so our friends took up the slack helping to care for our children.

Our local parish started a round the clock prayer vigil. Johanna's baptismal dress, used just six weeks before she was diagnosed, hung from the altar as a sign of new life.

Still, with all the prayer and positive thinking, the prevailing sentiments were ones of tragedy and death. Every time a doctor or nurse came into the room, there were conversations about the large tumor and introductions to the oncologist who would follow her after the tumor was resected. If we were so aware of the negative outlook, I began to wonder if Johanna was too.

I decided to ask God what He thought of this perspective. In the midst of it all, of course we were praying, seemingly unceasingly. With every breath and sigh, tear and momentary smile, there was a petition for healing for my baby. But I hadn't really asked God what He was thinking. Most people wouldn't bother, but for me it's a way of life.

Sometimes in these types of crises, people turn away from faith in God. It's totally understandable. The age old question, "If God is a loving God, then why do good people suffer?" rears its ugly and suspicious head quickly when one is faced with the suffering of an innocent child. Many people choose to turn away in anger rather than seek God's perspective.

For me, turning away from God in the midst of a crisis is like shutting the door on my trusted friend, wisest parent and the abiding lover of my soul. In each of those relationships, there are certainly times of intense hurt and anger, maybe even feelings of betrayal. But to turn away completely is like losing a part of oneself. I needed all of me to deal with all of this. I knew I needed the Lord to help us through.

Through worship, I came to know God's heart and experience His love for me in a deeply personal way. In college, I learned the sweet discipline of daily prayer and reflection on scripture. I learned how to listen for God's voice, and I started to keep a journal.

I have been journaling for over 30 years now. I started it as a therapeutic writing exercise when I was in high school. In college, I learned to use journaling to aid me in prayer and reflection as I recorded my thoughts, scriptures and personal words from God that struck my heart and fed my soul. Now, I have volumes of journals, which recount a journey of God's faithful love.

So in this troubled time, turning away from this avenue of grace I had come to enjoy through daily prayer was not an option. Rather than out of obligation, prayer became my lifeline, tossed out into the ocean waves, to gently guide me to the shore.

As I sat next to my Johanna with the crib rail down, I grabbed her tiny fingers and stroked her little head that now had a large tube coming out of it. She was covered in sterile dressing, and betadine colored her skin to give the appearance of blood. It was startling to look at, but in the midst, she gave us sweet smiles.

Knowing that my husband was going to bring my children soon, I wanted to take this time to pray for them, for us, for Johanna. I needed to hear God's heart on this struggle and have a sense of the plan that unfolded before us. While I normally don't play "Bible roulette," randomly opening scripture to get a word from God, this day I decided to do just that. I needed this word to come from outside myself; I needed a direct Divine Intervention to guide our way.

I opened my bible to this scripture:

We have this treasure in jars of clay to show that this all-surpassing power is from God and not from us. We are hard pressed on every side, but not crushed; perplexed, but not in despair; persecuted, but not abandoned; struck down, but not destroyed. We always carry around in our body the death of Jesus, so that the life of Jesus may also be revealed in our body…

We believe therefore we speak, knowing that the one who raised the Lord Jesus will raise us also with Jesus and place us in His presence. Everything is for you, that grace bestowed in abundance on more and more people may cause the thanksgiving to overflow for the glory of God.

Therefore, we are not discouraged; rather, although our outer self is wasting away, our inner self is being renewed day by day. For this momentary affliction is achieving for us an eternal weight of glory beyond all comparison, as we look not to what is seen but to what is unseen; for what is seen is transitory but what is unseen is eternal.

2 Corinthians 4:7-10, 13, 15-18

I was profoundly moved by this reading and quickly realized that this was indeed a promise and a blueprint for the why and the how of this present struggle. The treasure in earthen vessels presumes frailty and vulnerability that requires one to look to God for strength. This scripture "lifted the veil" on the way to suffer in communion with Jesus.

In this word, God did not promise me that the pain would go away; actually I was assured of afflictions and persecutions. But in the midst of those, the death and resurrection of Jesus would get us through. God promised me in these verses, which I renamed *Johanna's Scripture*, that grace would abound to overflow on more and more people.

Finally, God gave me exactly what I asked for. I asked for God's perspective and He summed it up in this:

> *For this momentary affliction is achieving for us an eternal weight of glory beyond all comparison, as we look not to what is seen but to what is unseen; for what is seen is transitory but what is unseen is eternal.*
>
> 2 Corinthians 4:17

That one verse says it all. If we grasp this, we question nothing. Every affliction, every difficulty achieves a greater purpose of leading us deeper through that which is seen to that which is unseen. I realized this little baby who was scheduled to have her second brain surgery in four days was much more than a suffering child in need of intervention. Johanna was a sign and promise of hope, an icon of resurrection, and a pledge of the eternal life that is to come.

With this renewed perspective, I prepared for my children's visit. Before they came in, I met them in the parking lot. It was unseasonably warm for mid-November. I will never forget the walk we took on the pathways surrounding the hospital.

When I saw them, they ran to greet me, and I hugged each of them.

They seemed so old to me now. They had lots of questions and concerns about their baby sister and when was she coming home.

My daughter MaryAngela melted into me to snuggle. She was just a baby herself; barely out of diapers, she still nursed occasionally before she went to sleep. Now she seemed like a giant. She was strong and secure with her dancing blue eyes, high cheekbones and sweet smile that brought joy to the sorrows of my heart. Anna, the little mother, rattled on about the things that were being done and how she was caring for Lady, our black lab puppy. She told me about the tricks she was teaching the puppy and showed me the beautiful picture she drew for her sister.

My son David was strong and pensive. Of all of them, he most understood the gravity of the situation. He was a great big brother, protective and caring to his little sisters, right from the beginning of their lives to this day. His eyes searched mine, looking for clues to the unstated question that whispered in his heart. Despite our jovial conversation and the walk, my wise son read between the lines of words that were spoken. It seemed to me that in one week David had left a part of his childhood behind so that he could support his little sisters and shelter them in the storm. Was that fair? I wondered. Yet, I knew I had no control over the new roles that were unfolding in our lives.

We brought the children into the PICU donning masks to ensure that they wouldn't be exposing their baby sister to anything that would delay the pending neurosurgery.

My little MaryAngela clung to me and refused a mask, placing her own hand over her mouth while she giggled and greeted baby Johanna. Her eyes lit up with excitement and she responded to the children's faces and their love.

David was encouraged by the interaction that he had waited so long to see. With the pressure in Johanna's brain controlled with the drain, she seemed closer to those milestones in the baby development chart. This made her older brother very happy.

Anna stroked Johanna's hands and played with her toes, delighted by her little sister's smile. At one point in the visit, I handed our camera to a friend of ours to take a family picture. At first, my friend stood frozen and motionless, stunned at the thought that this could be the last family picture we would take with Johanna. She wiped away her tear filled eyes and focused on serving us through this small task that meant so much to our little family.

We gathered around Johanna in the crib, and each of us placed our hands on her to say a prayer for healing. We asked God to protect Johanna and to bring her home to us soon. Then the kids each kissed Johanna goodbye. My husband and I hugged them and walked them out as they went back home with a friend. Another milestone was met that day.

Preparations for surgery continued as we met some of the doctors who would be in the operating room the next day. This mass in her brain had to be removed, but it also could move her brainstem in a way that would kill her. Realizing the gravity of the situation, we signed consent.

We were told that the pediatric neurosurgeon, who had been away at a conference, was returning early to be the head surgeon for Johanna's case. We were anxious to meet him and hear his perspective.

My husband had decided to stay the night with us in the PICU because Johanna was scheduled to be the first case and would likely be moved to the operating room by 6am. The surgeon arrived late that night and met with us in a tiny room where he showed us the MRI.

He examined Johanna briefly before our meeting and smiled as she kicked her little hands and feet to greet him. He was happy to learn that her responses were appropriate and that she was nursing well despite the challenges of the drains, lines and monitors that riddled her body and took up more space in the crib.

When we sat in the darkened room to view the large MRI scan before us, we were a little discouraged. This was the first time that my husband and I had a clear view of what was really going on inside our baby's brain. It was frightening. This tumor was large and seemed to take up the whole bottom and middle of her brain. The neurosurgeon showed us how the tumor was compressing her brainstem and explained the risks of the surgery. But then he shared with us a totally new perspective.

He suggested that although this scan was frightening and ominous, Johanna was telling us otherwise. The neurosurgeon asked us more questions about Johanna's reactions before the fluid in her brain was controlled and afterwards. Then he smiled and conveyed to us that he believed that this was not a cancerous tumor. He thought it might not be as involved as it appeared and that he could possibly remove the whole thing.

It struck me that this surgeon was *looking beyond what was seen to what was unseen*. The observation that Johanna was becoming more appropriate when the pressure was relieved in her brain indicated to him that she would be even better when this was removed. This was the first good news we had heard since beginning this journey four days earlier. He asked us to remain hopeful and to rest for the day ahead.

My husband and I were amazed. As I reread *Johanna's Scripture* which now hung above her head on the crib, I acknowledged that it was already coming to pass. The neurosurgeon looked beyond what was seen to things unseen by others. He believed and therefore he spoke, and we were filled with abundant grace and hope.

My husband and I slept in chairs next to our daughter's crib. I had one that reclined a little. He sat up most of the night. We took turns drifting off to sleep and being wide-awake. We said very little to each other in words, but much in glances and gestures while we watched Johanna sleep. At one point, I recall waking up and seeing Steve leaning over the crib, his head pressed against the bars of the crib and his hands outstretched over Johanna in prayer. He was praying aloud in tongues, a prayer language described in the book of Romans:

> *The Spirit comes to aid us in our weakness; for we do not know how to pray as we ought, but the Spirit itself intercedes with inexpressible groaning. And the One who searches hearts knows what is the intention of the Spirit, because it intercedes for the holy ones according to God's will.*
> Romans 8:26-27

Steve wasn't just praying; he was groaning in the Spirit for the will of God to be made manifest in our daughter. My heart rested secure in knowing the Lord would answer the groaning of my husband's heart according to the will of God.

I guess we finally drifted off to sleep because a few hours later I awoke, sat in the rocking chair and held Johanna in my arms. As I prayed from the depths of my heart, God broke the stillness of that quiet night. I heard in a whisper: "*I can take her now and her pain will end, or, she can live now, but it will be a hard road ahead. Which do you choose?*"

As I look back on those words, I sometimes wonder how and why it was that God seemed to include me in a decision of life and death. It almost seemed like we had a choice, but in truth, we know that the Lord alone is the Author of Life who holds the future in His hands.

However in every great move of God in scripture, a choice is to be made. God asks us to cooperate with His grace and never forces His will on us. And likewise, whatever He asks, He always provides. God asked me a question, and the Spirit gave me the answer as I replied, "I choose the path of miracles!" My voice echoed in the dark of that hospital room.

I believed, therefore I spoke.

2 Corinthians 4:14

My proclamation met the dawn, and the day began with nurses getting my daughter ready for the surgery ahead. Friends began to gather in the waiting area outside our room as Steve and I got ready for another long and vitally important day. We were confident and ready for whatever lay ahead.

By the time the surgeon walked into the room for the final consent, at least ten people were gathered by Johanna's bedside. He went over some last minute details and asked us if we had any more questions—we had one.

Though we didn't know if he believed in God or if he had any inclinations to prayer, we asked the neurosurgeon if we could pray with him before we brought Johanna to surgery. He agreed to prayer and bowed his head.

My husband and I placed our hands on the doctor's shoulders as we prayed for the anointing of the Holy Spirit to come upon him. We prayed for his wisdom, strength and endurance. As we prayed over the doctor, I knew that we were giving God permission to use this man to save our daughter's life. It was a commissioning. We were anointing and affirming him for a special mission. Our baby's life was in God's hands, and God's hands placed her in the hands of this neurosurgeon.

We began our path of miracles that day, unsure of very little except that we knew Who was in control. The surgery, a nearly complete resection of the tumor, went very well. When the neurosurgeon emerged from the operating room, he was cautiously optimistic. The tumor appeared to be some type of large hemorrhagic material that no one could identify as yet. It probably wasn't cancerous and it might not grow back.

Even though it seemed benign, the tumor destroyed the left lobe of Johanna's cerebellum. The little that was left of that part of the brain was removed. The neurosurgeon seemed optimistic that this event would melt away as a bad memory. Hopefully the interventions were done and would yield to the possibility of a normal life for our infant daughter.

While we rejoiced in this news, the words spoken to me in the middle of the night about the hard road ahead echoed in my mind and heart. They were not words of discouragement, but rather of caution with hope. I took them to mean that we would need to prepare for the long haul. Rather than seeing this time as a really tough sprint, we needed to plan for a marathon that could last Johanna's lifetime.

The next heat of the marathon began when Johanna had her surgery for the placement of a shunt in her brain only one month after the first brain surgery. The tumor had destroyed the natural pathways for the fluid to flow. She needed a shunt to drain the fluid from her brain into her abdomen.

In the next year, Johanna was diagnosed with cerebellar dysfunction, balance difficulties and vision problems resulting from the destruction of one of the lobes of the cerebellum. This dysfunction also affects her motor and cognitive skills.

She did not learn to sit up until she was almost a year old, and she was over two when she learned to walk. In her first year of life, she had six brain surgeries because of shunt malfunctions. Whereas some parents can't wait for the closing of their baby's soft spot on the top of the head, we were grateful for the additional space it afforded the changes in the pressure in Johanna's brain. Her soft spot was another means of assessing her symptoms. It would become tight or bulge when the pressure was high, or soft and squishy when the shunt was flowing properly.

Johanna's second Christmas was far less eventful than her first, and we imagined that we might enjoy the holidays with our new little family of four children; now eleven, eight, four and 18 months. That seemed likely until New Year's Eve. As the world welcomed 1998 with cheers of Auld Lang Syne, we sat back in the PICU hovering over our toddler with caution. She cried and vomited, exhibiting signs of changes in her brain. It was a stark reminder that time was not our own.

On the first day of 1998, we were told that Johanna had numerous bleeds in her brain caused by a condition called cerebral cavernous angiomas or CCM's. Now we knew for sure that the tumor she was born with was part of a neurological disease. But there was very little known about this disease. One neurologist gave us a copy of the one medical journal article that was written on the topic.

The hard road ahead was becoming apparent, and to some it seemed anything but miraculous. But to me, it was a journey of faith along the path of miracles.

CHAPTER THREE

THE DREAM

After Johanna was born and diagnosed with this rare neurological disease, our lives were never the same. Everything seemed so different than what we had known. We had a plan for our life. Now we were not sure where we were headed.

Before Johanna, life was very busy with ministry work, homeschooling and raising three children. We worked very hard to afford our first home in the middle of Long Island. We had wanted to move further east, to a more rural area of Long Island's East End. But we couldn't afford it, and it seemed so impractical because so much of my husband's job took him all over the island. Rather than bemoaning the fact that we couldn't move to the farm, we decided to make the farm where we lived. We lived on a corner lot with a half-acre of fenced in yard. We planted vegetables, sunflowers, and zinnias and even made a formal gated garden to spend quiet nights outside. We had an above ground pool for hours of play in the summer. My husband built a large fort from slotted wood so that the kids could scale the walls or climb the ladder to the 10-foot deck above. It was an adventurous place to live for young children.

In those years before Johanna, my husband and I grew in tremendous ways. We spent long romantic evenings talking about our future, our concerns for our children and planning for ways we could care for them better. Ministry in the church was very busy and homeschooling took a lot of time, but we still found time for each other and for our family. However, the busier we got with the work of the Lord and raising kids, the more it seemed we forgot the Lord. We seemed to be living a perfect life for a young family. But deep within me, I knew something was missing. There was a depth of holiness that we seemed to be lacking.

One day I found myself praying, "Lord, do whatever you need to do to make us truly holy."

As we approached the 10th anniversary of our engagement, we celebrated by conceiving our fourth baby. Over the years, we used natural family planning and breastfeeding to space our children. Although it required some discipline, it enhanced our relationship and helped to keep us open to God's creative plan for our lives. We renewed our wedding vows on our tenth anniversary while Johanna kicked in my womb. She was born a month later—our anniversary gift to one another and to our children.

Prior to Johanna's birth, I had imagined that we would be going on a lot of field trips and having amazing homeschooling adventures together. I had thought that life would be one new discovery after another. Before Johanna, I built our school curriculum around unit studies. We all studied the same subject at different grade levels; it was the same concept as a one room school-house. After Johanna was diagnosed, I realized a prepared curriculum which the kids could easily take to someone else's home or to the hospital was going to be the best way for us to continue homeschooling. It wasn't quite as creative, but we adapted the tools to fit our new life.

Though my attentions were divided and I was frequently staying in the hospital with Johanna, my children grew in different and more beautiful ways than I had imagined.

My son, David, imagined great battles and practiced his protective survival skills in our backyard. He was always devising schemes for spying on the criminals (real ones) on the other side of the fence. He learned about drugs as we watched deals taking place in the dead end beside our property. He asked a lot of very specific questions about these deals and about the kids involved; he was always concerned that our family was safe. He learned from the vigilant efforts of his father how to protect our family. Many times, as I tucked him in to sleep at night, my tough son would look me in the eye and whisper, "Is Johanna going to die?"

My eldest daughter, Anna was a sweet and caring little girl who loved to sing and dance and imagine amazing playful scenes with her dolls and Lego people. Her imaginary adventures included large prayer meetings with Barbie, babies born to married and single moms, and a host of characters being launched into space to travel to the moon! She was very sensitive to the needs of her baby sister, as she remarked, "Mommy, it's been hard to see Johanna go through all this stuff, but isn't it wonderful that we got to keep her as a baby just a little bit longer?"

MaryAngela was and is my little warrior. Even before Johanna was born, she exuded strength and resilience. She was an easy-going and fiercely independent child. She was a lot of fun! MaryAngela climbed furniture before she could walk and kept up with her older brother in all the backyard battles. From the very beginning of her life, MaryAngela had an excitement and a glow about her that was palpable. On her fourth birthday, as we were looking through her baby book, she asked, "Mommy, was this before my brain surgery or after my brain surgery?" My little girl, who was just three when her baby sister had her first surgery, thought that all babies had brain surgeries. It took me a year to realize that's what she thought.

Two years after Johanna was born and diagnosed, we sat at a family retreat, exhausted, but trying to spend time reconnecting as a young family. The first two years were a never ending blur of hospitals, doctors and consultations from around the country, trying to figure out the rare pieces to this puzzle in Johanna's brain. This family retreat gave us time to reflect on this path of miracles and how we all fit into the plan.

We sat discussing the question, "What are some of the gifts God gives your family to build your faith?"

My pre-adolescent son, wise beyond his years, answered, "Well that's obvious." With that all knowing kid look, he continued, "Johanna is God's gift to us to help us grow in our faith."

I filled up with tears knowing that the Lord was truly answering my prayer. Holiness sat in my arms, nursed at my breast and tugged at my jeans for attention. Holiness called from the little ones who surrounded me each day with their endless questions and inquisitive minds. We didn't need much retreat time or to read a lot of books. Holiness was happening in our day to day life.

The local parish community and the neighborhood surrounded and supported us throughout the early years of Johanna's birth and diagnosis. Neighbors and friends brought meals, helped care for our older three kids and cleaned the house. It was an exceptional time of camaraderie. The shock of the first two years of Johanna's life and the surgeries totaling ten, gave us little time to focus on the details of home.

While we loved where we lived, we also struggled with the proximity to a major shopping plaza that brought a lot of foot traffic just outside our door. The drug deals increased, and one night my husband interrupted an assault on a young girl. Troubled teens flocked to the dead-end next to our home. We called the police a few times a week for dumpster fires and disturbances. One night a drugged and drunk teenager slammed his fist and then his whole body into our front picture window to threaten us for calling the police.

Some of these problems preceded Johanna's birth, but the stress of managing life with a medically fragile child intensified the feeling of being trapped in a very difficult living situation. It was hard knowing that our older children were now left in the care of friends and sitters in our home and that sometimes they weren't safe. After years of trying to close off the walkway that led to the shopping center next to our home and complaining to town officials to no avail, we were getting discouraged.

One morning, I had all four kids in tow, and we headed out for less than an hour to run some errands. I came home to find that someone had broken into our home. Drawers were ransacked and small items were stolen. I felt violated and very frightened. It was apparent, because I was gone with the children for such a short time, that someone had been watching the house and had seen us leave. This was the final straw. We set our sights on moving to the North Fork of Long Island.

We had some very dear friends who lived out on the North Fork, and we visited them often. We were close enough to be godparents to each other's children. We celebrated birthdays and some holidays together and especially enjoyed the fall pumpkin season out on the North Fork.

I remember one particularly difficult time when Johanna had a few brain surgeries only months apart. We were visiting our North Fork friends, and I decided to take a walk, pushing Johanna in the stroller. I looked down at her head, riddled with scars, as the wind swirled around us in the open skies. Everywhere I looked, the sky was bright, blue and beautiful. The clouds were an ever-changing dimension, and the sun warmed my face.

On that walk, I poured out my heart—and my tears—making a pact with God. I told God that despite the challenges, I willingly and lovingly received this child as a special blessing from heaven. But I also reminded the Lord that we needed a home where we felt safe and where we could experience the healing power of creation.

I am a firm believer that being out in the elements in all seasons is an integral strategy for living a healthy and holy life. In our little ranch home we had done our best to bring the farm to us. But there were no views of the sunsets and sunrises. We rarely saw the stars. I knew we needed to find or build a home on the North Fork—just so I could see the sky. At times, living life with chronic disease can feel like you are being suffocated. Being outside, under a big sky, gives me perspective and helps me to trust that tomorrow will be a better day.

After I shared my vision with my husband, we decided that we would only look at homes with a view of the North Fork sky. The North and South Forks split out from Long Island which extends about 80 miles from Manhattan. We are surrounded by water on Long Island: the Long Island Sound to the North, the Atlantic Ocean to the South, and the Peconic Bay between the Forks. The South Fork is the Hamptons—beautiful and very busy with the lifestyles of the rich and famous. We started spending our weekends looking at houses, and we put our home on the market.

The North Fork is an older and more rural community setting. There is an abundance of farmlands and vineyards. In the fifteen years that we have lived here, the Long Island Wine Country has been gleaning a national reputation for their fine wines and bucolic scenery that is a tourist destination year round. As we looked for a home, I knew that we couldn't touch expensive water view properties near the Sound or the Bay. So we looked in the middle of the North Fork, and we found our sky. We discovered some lots that we could build on and looked for a contractor who was willing to build a modular home.

In the midst of our search, during the fall of Johanna's second year, she had a major bleed in the middle of her brain from one of the cavernous angiomas. She was losing control of her left side and suffering from seizures. We ended up in New York City for the surgery. The cavernoma was deep in her brain. We were very nervous about what could happen. When she woke up from the surgery, she struggled to speak, and it took a long time for her to recover. In the midst of it, we poured over house plans and prayed for provision.

It took months for her, and us, to recover from that surgery. Then just before the holidays, Johanna's shunt malfunctioned again, adding insult to injury and requiring another surgery which brought her lifetime total to ten in the first two and a half years. By Thanksgiving, we were exhausted as we prepared for Christmas. I was feeling compelled to move our little family despite the onslaught of difficulties. But a move was becoming less likely as the months went on.

On one of our weekend house searches, we purchased our Christmas tree at a farm on the North Fork. In the Christmas shop at the tree farm, I noticed that they were holding a raffle for a ceramic house. At home we had a small display of holiday ceramic houses. The raffle was a fundraiser for Ronald McDonald House, and the sign on the ceramic house displayed their tagline: "The House that Love Built." I filled up with tears when I purchased the raffle ticket because we had just stayed at the Ronald McDonald House in New York City while Johanna was in the hospital there. The house provided us with a safe place where my husband and I could take turns staying with the kids and visiting Johanna in the hospital.

As I cradled Johanna in my arms, her tiny tiara of staples from her most recent brain surgery glistened next to the tinseled Christmas trees. I tearfully handed my money to the cashier in exchange for a raffle ticket, very aware that Ronald McDonald House was the perfect charity for us to donate to this Christmas season. We loaded the tree and the kids back into the car and headed home to decorate.

The next day, we sat on our couch and admired our newly decorated Christmas tree. It took up about half of our living room. In that magic moment, our children asked us what we wanted for Christmas. Amidst the usual musings about toys and fun, our children each expressed that what they most wanted for Christmas was for Johanna not to have any more brain surgeries. I agreed.

After that, the kids pressed me for another special Christmas wish. They quipped, "Mommy, what do you want Santa to bring you?"

I gazed at the tree and replied, "All I want under the tree for Christmas is a North Fork house."

My children burst out in peals of laughter at the silliness of their crazy mom's request. I laughed, even as I whispered reminding the Lord, Santa, and whoever else was listening, that I really wanted to move to the North Fork.

Christmas came and went without another trip to the hospital and with visits from friends and family. It was nice to be home. The day after Christmas we headed east for our annual Christmas celebration with our North Fork friends. Right before we left our house, the phone rang and it was the Christmas Tree Farm calling to tell us that we had won the raffle for "The House that Love Built!" The kids were very excited as we poured into the car and headed east. Our first stop was the Christmas Tree Farm.

When we arrived at the Christmas shop, we excitedly told the clerk that we were the winners of the raffle. Then, the owner came over and helped pack the beautiful ceramic house. As they were packing it up, we told them the story of why we purchased the raffle—how we had spent some time at Ronald McDonald House in NYC during Johanna's major brain surgery. We told them about her situation as Johanna smiled coyly, snuggled into my arms. We thanked the owner and the clerks as they filled up with tears. Then we headed to our Christmas celebration.

When we arrived home later that evening, tired and happy from a full day of Christmas cheer, I looked around the living room to find a place to put our new ceramic house. Since it was larger than the ones that decorated our mantle, my husband and I decided to plug it in and place it underneath the Christmas tree as a central part of our decorations.

We tucked the kids into bed and headed back towards the living room. As my husband and I glanced at the tree, the two of us were suddenly struck with the compelling image before us. We were stopped dead in our tracks as we realized that my Christmas wish was granted!

All I wanted for Christmas was a North Fork house under my Christmas tree. There it was before my eyes; literally, a house from the North Fork was sitting under our Christmas tree! We laughed as we called the kids out from their bedrooms. We gathered them on the couch to soak up the image before our eyes. We joked about how literal God and Santa must be. We realized that this was a clear sign that God was answering our prayer to move to the North Fork. That little house was a promise, that in time it was all going to work out. That day we knew for sure that we would soon be moving to the North Fork.

Three months later, we sold our house and were in contract to build a modular home in Jamesport, a quaint village on the North Fork. As the house plans were shaping up, it occurred to us how similar they were to the ceramic "House that Love Built ." We decided to go with the same yellow siding, green shutters and red door that were the colors of the ceramic house. We moved into our new home the day before Thanksgiving and eleven months after our Christmas wish was granted. The House that Love Built lit up the entryway to our new house that love built! It served as a precious reminder that God hears our prayers.

We settled into our North Fork life very well. Thanks to the Make a Wish Foundation, Johanna had an above ground pool that gave hours and hours of fun in the summer. We became part of the local community. We continued homeschooling and enjoyed visiting local historical sites and living life on our little farm. Our neighbors even had horses that we could see from our backyard.

Though our home life changed, the surgeries continued. Johanna's shunt malfunctioned a lot. The cavernous angiomas in her brain continued to multiply and hemorrhage. Each time they did, it was like she suffered a small stroke. Our home became a day hospital, with therapists in and out the door. Johanna went to preschool for a little while to get some of her therapies at a school near our home. But when it came time for kindergarten, we realized that the safest place for a child who is medically fragile with special needs was home with her family. So Johanna joined our homeschool, and she thrived on the attention she got from her brother and sisters.

Soon after we moved to Jamesport, we were in the hospital for most of the summer. Johanna developed a yeast infection in her brain. My husband Steve was always amazing at entertaining Johanna and the kids and doing crafts with all of them. He decorated her IV poles, especially for the holidays (we hit them all). But by far, his most creative craft was the barn he and Johanna made out of tongue depressors. All the kids in the playroom were asking if they could make one, and all the moms just rolled their eyes at my husband.

The tongue depressor craft was a prototype for a barn that my husband wanted to build in our backyard. We needed a garage but couldn't afford one. A barn was a cheaper option and by far cooler in our farm setting. The next summer, he built the barn, and Johanna was well enough to help paint it. Despite the trials, we had to keep going. We strove to live life to the fullest for our family. It wasn't perfect by any means, but there was a whole lot of love.

Along with the surgeries and the normal life that we struggled to maintain, my water nightmares continued for years after Johanna was born. Sometimes they served as a warning sign that we were entering into a period of extreme difficulties.

The scenes of the nightmares changed from time to time. They always centered on the ocean, and I always had a sense of helplessness. Very often the dreams began with a fun day at the beach for our family. But then a tsunami would ensue and sweep our little family out to the ocean. In the dream, my husband and I struggled to save the children; I had the younger two in my arms as the waves carried us out to sea. But more often, the nightmares were exactly the same one that I had for weeks after Johanna's birth. I was out in the middle of the ocean in a stormy sea. There was no land in sight, and I was treading water with Johanna in my arms.

Then one time there was a significant change in that familiar nightmare. I saw the same frightening visage, but this time I heard a voice. I immediately knew it was God. His voice called out to me from the heavens. It was clear, calm and quiet above the lapping waters.

God spoke, *"You can let go. You are in the ocean of My Mercy. You will feel like you are drowning as the ocean waters rise over your heads. But I will teach you a new way of breathing—how to breathe underwater."*

This word gave me a new perspective on our trials. In that moment, the cold threatening ocean, which I thought was filled with untold dangers, became a place where I could rest. I did not have to keep treading water because God's love and mercy, indeed, His very presence, was surrounding me in the midst of the trials.

I understood in that moment, that it was quite possible that my daughter's struggles were never going to end, at least not in this lifetime. It was nice to think that I could keep our heads above water, but as the nightmares continued year after year, it was apparent to me that sometimes treading water is just too hard. I often felt like I was beginning to drown. But now I could let go. I could trust. God promised to teach me a new way to breathe—to breathe underwater.

As if to confirm the dream and bring it out from my subconscious, the very next day, I had an experience with Johanna while we were swimming. Johanna stood on the deck of our above ground pool. That day, Johanna had no life jacket on and she boldly asked, "Mommy, can I jump in and swim to you?"

The dream and the voice were foremost in my mind. Intrigued by the timing of this request, I nodded and said, "I'm here." My little girl dove into the water and swam beneath the surface, all with one breath. She emerged with great excitement from beneath the water. She was proud and I was amazed. It was the first time ever that she swam underwater. For her, it was a proud moment; for me it was a sign. Her feat was a confirmation of that life-changing dream and a seal of the promise that the Lord would teach us a new way of breathing—underwater.

I wrote that dream down in my journal. In the weeks and months ahead, I reflected on the dream. I realized that God was unveiling a plan for a future full of hope. My circumstances did not change; in fact, they got much harder. But now I had a new hope. The knowledge that I was not alone in that dark ocean, but rather enveloped in the ocean of God's mercy, gave me courage to face the days and years ahead. For so many years, I thought I had to keep going through the next crisis by holding my breath or treading water to stay afloat.

I now realized that life was frequently more than I could handle. When the burdens of life and caregiving become too much for me and I feel like I am drowning, I simply remember to let go and *BREATHE*.

Letting go when circumstances threaten to overtake your life can feel a lot like drowning. However, the more I let go, the better I learned how to *BREATHE*.

As a writer and somewhat of a mystic, I think in metaphors and allegories. I like to use acronyms to help me focus. As I reflected on this dream and our journey, this acronym came to mind:

B - *Believe*

R - *Restore*

E - *Engage*

A - *Advocate*

T - *Time*

H - *Hope*

E - *Endure*

People always ask me how I survive and thrive in the midst of these trials. As this acronym came to life, I realized I had a way to share the lessons I have learned about letting go and breathing underwater. First, I wrote a talk, then a seminar. Finally, I can share them in this book.

In the subsequent chapters, I share my journey through the lens of this dream and this acronym. It is my hope that if you are struggling to keep your head above the water, that you will find the courage to let go and just breathe.

The Spirit of God has made me; the breath of the Almighty gives me life.

Job 33:4

CHAPTER FOUR

BELIEVE

If you want to learn to breathe underwater, you must believe.

Before Johanna was born, I enjoyed play dates at the beach. I was a decent swimmer, having taught myself how to swim when I was growing up and then taking formal lessons in high school. The past eighteen years, I have taken a different kind of swimming lesson. It has little to do with strokes and everything to do with breathing.

The challenges of my life—raising a medically fragile child, economic crises, and everyday stress—have often felt like pounding ocean waves that threaten to pull me under. All of us can relate to this image. You do not have to experience the kinds of trials that I have to relate to this feeling of drowning under circumstances. Each of us faces circumstances in our lives that cause us to feel overwhelmed. When we find ourselves in over our heads, we only have three options: work really hard to keep your head above water, drown in our circumstances, or let go and breathe. I chose to breathe, but first I had to believe.

The holidays were particularly tough times to plan for, especially with four young children. I recall one year we made it through Christmas without a hospitalization. I was feeling on top of my game, so I decided to plan a small get together for New Year's Eve. But somewhere in between Christmas and News Year, Johanna started falling a lot. She seemed kind of disorientated, like she lost a sense of her body in space. I noticed that when she ate, she played with her tongue. She also started having some serious hiccups. All these things sound like regular incidences with a young child. But when you have a child like Johanna, you have to read between the lines.

We ended up going for a brain MRI. I figured that things couldn't be that bad if the technician let us go home. When we got home, I set to planning this party. By gosh, we were going to get all the way through the holidays if it killed me. Early in the day on New Year's Eve, I got a call from the neurosurgeon. The MRI showed a new cavernoma in the pons, the top of the brainstem, in the deepest part of the brain. Not only was it new, it was hemorrhaging. The falling and swallowing problems, the hiccups and the rolling of the tongue, all made sense to me now. But other than that, she seemed relatively okay. Our doctor suggested that we take her to a hospital in New York City. I cringed, both because the City on New Year's Eve was not a place you wanted to be driving to and because I was determined to get through the holidays.

I promised him that we would watch her carefully and if she showed any serious neurological decline, especially if her breathing changed or she started vomiting, we would call 911 and head straight to the hospital. He was a little reticent, but he trusted my abilities to keep her safe. He contacted the doctors in NYC and told them to expect us in the ER the day after New Year's. Now I felt like I had a little more control.

As the night went on, I watched Johanna with a decided diligence. I stopped giving her regular food and moved her to a soft mechanical diet, making sure that the consistency of her food was thick and mushy, so that she wouldn't choke. I kept her at my side at all times, and I never relaxed. Yes, we were home for the holidays, and I was freaking out.

While my family enjoyed their New Year's Eve, I sat distracted with

Johanna on my lap; I slept with her in my arms. When we got up the next day, we made plans for the other kids, and we took her to the hospital. We almost made it through the holidays. I thought that maybe we could be home for the Feast of Epiphany, or Little Christmas. It didn't seem to matter anymore. I just didn't want her to die over Christmas.

In the ICU, they placed her on monitors and put a tube in her nose to start her on total liquid nutrition. I went from control to drowning. Over the next few days, there were conversations with neurosurgeons from around the country. Everyone said that this cavernoma was inoperable. But it was hemorrhaging and it was large. It seemed we had no options, and that I had no control. While my husband stayed most days with our other kids, I sat beside Johanna's bed, praying for a better outcome. The days turned into a week, and the Feast of Epiphany was just one day away. Controlling my circumstances felt like treading water, and you can only do that so long before you feel like you are drowning.

My husband and I decided it was better for the kids to celebrate Little Christmas with some friends. A lovely family with lots of kids was having a celebration on the eve of Little Christmas including a Mass at their home and a big dinner. I asked them to pray for Johanna, who at this point could not speak and was beginning to withdraw into an eerie silence as she drifted off to sleep.

I stayed at her bedside and prayed. Then I had this vision, kind of like a picture that painted in my mind. I saw angels, Mary, and Jesus himself walk into Johanna's room. It was like there was a heavenly prayer meeting going on all around us. I knew that God was telling me to expect an "Epiphany," a manifestation of God in Johanna's life.

I so wanted to believe this word and the picture that was playing out in my mind's eye. But I was drowning in these overwhelming circumstances and in despair. I looked at my little girl who seemed so far away and unreachable as this inoperable cavenoma hemorrhaged in the deepest part of her brain. What choice did I have? Treading water and control didn't work. Drowning seemed to be my only option. But instead I took the first step to breathe; *I chose to believe!*

As I closed my eyes to sleep, I felt like I was off duty. The picture of Jesus, Mary and the angels praying over my little girl gave me comfort enough to let go and believe.

In the middle of the night, I heard Johanna call my name. I sprang to my feet and looked at her in amazement as she said "Mommy, I have to go to the bathroom." When I looked closer I realized that the nasal-gastric tube was pulled out. Johanna was quite lucid as she expressed that she needed to go to the bathroom. I rang for the nurse who came immediately. She was also was astonished that Johanna was so responsive. We helped her to the bathroom and immediately noticed that her balance was better. She was her regular chatty self.

The nurse remarked, "This is miraculous!" I agreed and thought to myself, "if you only knew." When we got back to the bed, the nurse found the tube that somehow was no longer in Johanna's nose or feeding into her stomach. Prior to this, it had been firmly taped in, and because Johanna fears tearing tape off and pulling tubes out, I doubted that she actually pulled it out. I secretly wondered if one of those angels decided she didn't need it anymore.

The nurse said that given the dramatic change in Johanna's condition, she needed to be reevaluated in the morning to decide if they would put the tube back in. It seemed to her that Johanna had turned an unexpected corner. It would have been unexpected to me too—except that I chose to believe.

Johanna chatted sleepily as we drifted back to sleep, both of us breathing deep sighs of relief. The next morning the neurologists came in and noted Johanna's remarkable progress. They planned to get a brain scan later that day. In the meantime, they thought it was a good idea to give her a light breakfast to see if she could eat and drink on her own.

While Johanna was eating, I called my husband and I put her on the phone. She said, "Hi Daddy, I'm eating breakfast." These were the first words she had spoken in almost a week. After they chatted for a few minutes, she handed me the phone. My husband could barely speak to me he was so moved.

I told him about the vision I had as I was going off to sleep. I told him how I saw Mary and Jesus and angels coming in to pray with Johanna and that the Lord promised that we would witness a miracle. As I spoke, Johanna interrupted me; and in her cute little voice she said, "Mommy, I had the same dream! I saw Jesus, Mary and Joseph and the angels come to my bedside to pray with me. But then I also saw the three Kings. They came in too. It was like a big parade." She knew that God was doing a miracle. She explained that she had the dream, and then she woke up to go to the bathroom.

My husband and I were astonished. Another amazing detail was that I specifically did not mention Little Christmas to Johanna. I didn't want her to feel sad that we wouldn't be celebrating Little Christmas with our family. In the ICU, there were no remaining signs of Christmas. The Three Kings in her dream were a sign of Epiphany—a manifestation of God.

The bleed in her brain stabilized and the swelling receded. She went from being in critical condition to stable, overnight. Johanna was released from the hospital 48 hours after Epiphany. A manifestation of God occurred right there in that hospital room. Both Johanna and I were given the ability to see it happen. All we needed was to believe.

The first step to breathing underwater is to believe. Lessons like these have taught me this essential truth. I was in a disposition to believe. Like the Three Kings of Epiphany, I spent my life seeking an answer and searching for the manifestation of God. When it arrived in a vision at my daughter's bedside, I believed. In the midst of this incredibly stressful time, I could have chosen to control the situation with worry, and then drown in my fear. Instead I chose to let go and believe.

The funny thing about learning to breathe underwater is that initially, belief and drowning feel the same. When people drown, the struggle ends. They are just too tired to keep fighting to keep their heads above the water.

Belief is like that; when we are tired of treading water, belief comes as an invitation to let go and surrender—to trust that we are in the ocean of mercy. First we believe and then we breathe.

Belief is essential for anyone who wants to get through any crisis or achieve any goal in life. We have to believe in ourselves to accomplish our purpose in life; we have to believe in something else beyond ourselves to find that purpose. My something else is Someone Else—God.

My mother's recounting of how God saved me from death at my birth helped me to believe. From that young age, I believed that God intervenes and has a plan for our lives. That story and my mother's devotion helped me to believe that God saved my life for a purpose.

We all want to believe. Belief is essential to living. We all have to believe in something; even atheists have to believe. We all have to believe that we will wake up the next morning and a new day will begin. Atheists have to believe that they possess the answers within themselves which cause other people to find faith in God. Unlike people of faith, atheists believe in their own power to change their circumstances; or they have tapped into this secret of letting go which is truly the beginning of learning to believe. Even our secularized society wants to believe. Think of Macy's marketing at Christmas. Shimmering signs light up 34th Street—*BELIEVE*.

The most wonderful thing I have discovered about belief is that it is not limited by the circumstances before me. People always ask me how I can believe in a loving God when I have so many trials. Rather than give a long explanation on redemptive suffering (I can do that), I tell them it's all about belief. When we believe, we open a window to heaven. We rise above those circumstances, or advance in spite of them, and find a higher power and purpose in the struggles.

The basic foundation of belief is really quite simple. It comes down to these four points: God exists. God loves me. God created me for a purpose. God uses everything in my life for good.

I have known my friend Bernadette for over twenty years, but we have only become friends in the last two years. She is part of a women's ministry that I lead. She is also the mother of an adult son with special needs. This woman prays a lot, and she prays for me all the time. Everyone should have a friend like Bernadette. When she prays for me, God gives her messages for me. Those messages, though they don't always make sense to her, always speak directly to my heart.

One day as Bernadette was driving in her car while praying for me, she had an overwhelming sense of God's presence. She heard these words for me: "Blessed are those who do not see, but believe."

That same week, I was back in the PICU with my daughter. There were no cool manifestations of God that week. It was a tough time. Like many tough times before, all I had was belief. I had to believe though I could not see.

God's word, spoken to me through Bernadette, inspired me to believe. In stressful times like that, it feels like I don't have what it takes to climb another hurdle. I don't have the energy, the resources or the time to get through another trial. It would appear by circumstances that God just does not care and that I am drowning.

Rather than treading water or gasping for air, I choose the first step to breathe. I choose to believe. I believe that God exists even when my circumstances say He can't possibly be here. I believe that He loves me though it sometimes feels like He's left me. I believe that I was created for a purpose and that all these struggles will be used for good.

When I choose to believe in God rather than the pain of my circumstances, I discover that I am blessed. I have a sense of peace. I see things work together for good. All around me the trials press in like those ocean waters rising over my head. Belief allows me to see God's hand at work to trust Him, and to know that He loves me and is working out a beautiful plan and purpose right in the midst of trials. When the waters rise over my head, I believe. God is in control. I just believe and take a deep breath.

REFLECT

Maybe there is a way out. Maybe there is a life preserver or a big boat on the way ready to rescue you. Either way, you may be feeling too tired to keep treading water. Just let go and believe. I promise that when you believe, you will breathe. Believe.

• Where are you right now in your journey to belief?

• Do you feel like you are trying to keep your head above water, or are you drowning in your circumstances?

Lord, I do believe. Help my unbelief.
Mark 9:24

NOTES

CHAPTER FIVE

RESTORE

To believe is the essential foundation for learning how to keep breathing when trials rise over your head. The second strategy is to restore.

To restore something means to replace what has been lost. In breathing, we take in oxygen as we inhale and release carbon dioxide as we exhale—the foundation for all life. As we inhale, the oxygen fills our lungs and restores every cell in our bodies to keep us alive. How then, can one restore if we seem to be overcome by trials, unable to take a deep breath?

Restoration begins with rest. Learning how to breathe underwater means learning to rest even when the stresses of life threaten to overwhelm us; it is most important at those times. Our minds need to rest from the onslaught of information thrown at us. Our spirits need rest. We need time to relax and unwind, to reflect on the blessings of our life when all we see are the difficulties.

I am an early-to-bed and early-to-rise kind of person. My body requires a lot of sleep. Before I go to sleep, I let everything go and surrender myself into the Lord's hands. Then I wake up and spend my first hour in prayer and meditation. Hedging my sleep in prayer makes all the difference for me. Prayer restores my body, mind and spirit.

Breathing is an automatic response that seems incredibly simple. It is until it is not. Spending a fair amount of time in an ICU setting with my daughter over the past eighteen years, I have a deep appreciation for heart rate, respirations and the amount of oxygen in the blood. In the PICU, those numbers are monitored very carefully, and if something is amiss, an incessant beeping noise calls attention to the change in any of those rates.

When we need rest and restoration, our body, mind and spirit tells us, much like the beeping of those monitors in the PICU setting. When our bodies need rest, we get worn out and may succumb more easily to illnesses and diseases. Our minds get cluttered, especially with the amount of information and the rate in which it is thrown at us every day. We need time to unplug and rest in order to restore. Spiritual restoration goes a long way for bringing rest to our minds and bodies as well.

Fibromyalgia was one of those beeping alarms going off in my body. I suffered from it for about ten years. The pain and fatigue that plagued my body got worse when I was under stress. Given the chronic and emergent nature of my daughter's disease, my body has always felt the effects of stress. When Johanna turned ten, I realized that she was not going to outgrow this disease. That's when I applied for assistance from New York State and when I got a handicap sticker for my car. I also decided that I had to take better care of myself.

Around that time, I read some articles on detoxification. There are as many different ways to detoxify as there are doctors and programs. Science has proven that toxins are stored in fat cells in our bodies. These fat cells are produced by the body to keep the toxins away from the major organs. This made sense to me and I began to wonder if some of the ache in my body could be helped by cleansing.

I made a decision to eat better and exercise, and I started Isagenix, a nutritional cleanse program. The shakes helped to restore needed nutrients that were depleted in my body. The cleanse helped my body to release the toxins safely and effectively. Supplementing with Isagenix shakes and cleanse helped my body to heal from fibromyalgia. Ending this battle helped to clear my mind and increase my energy so I could make better decisions to restore my health.

I loved Isagenix so much that we started a home business selling the products. It became our launch pad into the entrepreneurial market and has helped us weather the whirl of economic storms that has hit so many families over the past eight years. It has been a great home business that helped to restore our financial stability, and it has afforded me the flexibility I needed as a full-time caregiver. When we experience restoration, it affects everything; our bodies and spirits and even our financial resources can experience restoration.

It is not easy to restore what has been lost when you feel like you are drowning. I also promise you with all of my heart that restoration begins with a simple decision to change your perspective. It's the old adage of the half-empty or half-full glass. Restoration emerges with a change in your perspective.

Over the years, I have lost a lot in these trials. I have lost time, money, relationships, opportunities and dreams. We almost lost our house, and our marriage suffered tremendously. If I count up all that I have lost, it would seem that there wouldn't be enough resources in this lifetime to restore them. When I count my losses, they hold more power over my perspective. But when I choose to count my blessings instead, every trial has a chance for restoration, to be used for a greater purpose. I choose to count my blessings.

We often think that restoration means to return something to its former state or beauty. When museums restore paintings, there is a painstaking process of cleaning with carefully chosen tools and chemicals so as to protect the natural beauty. When we think of restoring relationships, we often think of reconciling differences and finding ways to return to a former way of relating.

When our lives are under stress, we lose a lot. We might lose weight in an unhealthy way. Or we might gain weight by binge eating, unhealthy snacking, or just bad choices. We lose energy as the stressors drain us. We might lose hair, money, time and even a sense of who we are as a person. Some of these things cannot be recovered, but all these things can be restored, if only we can see our losses yielding a greater gain.

One of the first things I lost in the years after Johanna was diagnosed was my sense of our family's identity. I'm not sure if my husband and my children felt that, but I did.

I had a sense of who we were: a close-knit Catholic family with a deep commitment to each other and to our faith. I knew what that looked like and had hopes of what it would look like in the future. We spent a lot of time together, working, playing and praying as a family. There were plans, lots of plans, for celebrations, outings, and building a future full of hope together.

But the chronic and emergent nature of Johanna's disease greatly impacted all that and changed it in ways I didn't immediately realize. Some of the restoration of our family is only being revealed now: in the strength of character in my children, in their compassion and in their respect for others.

To experience restoration, you have to recognize that you lost something, and sometimes that which you lost can never be brought back. I remember the first time I realized that we lost time which was irreplaceable. It was in the first year. By that time, she already had three surgeries and we were admitted to the PICU for her fourth. The shunt in her brain was malfunctioning for the first time despite the fact that our neurosurgeon said lots of kids get a shunt and never need another one until they are adults. That has certainly not been our experience.

Staying in a PICU is a sad and inspiring experience. It's inspiring to see how the doctors and nurses care for their patients, how families can come together to support one another, and how communities learn to share their resources for a family in need. It's sad because the children there are very sick. Inevitably, there are children whose parents are not by their side, and there are a few who have no one.

Some parents both need to work full time and struggle with wanting to be with their child and needing the money to survive. Many of those children are those with a chronic illness which causes disabilities. Those are the families who come to visit once or twice during the day and leave the television on all night for the children when the parents leave. The nurses do the best they can to provide attention and emotional support while they care for the children's physical needs. These are the children who cry often and loudly during the night. I want to hold them all and care for their needs. It breaks my heart to watch them all alone.

When Johanna was just four months old, she was scheduled for another surgery, and we were waiting in her room for the transport team to take her to the operating room. There was a newborn baby on the floor who cried often. A newborn's cry is quite distinctive and alarming. God made them like that to evoke our attention and care for the baby who is totally dependent on others for survival. My milk let down in response to the baby's cries especially because I wasn't able to nurse Johanna before surgery. I picked Johanna up and bounced her as I listened, longing to comfort her, myself and that newborn baby.

I looked at my husband and asked, as I kissed Johanna's head, "She doesn't sound like that anymore, does she?" He shook his head *no* as tears welled up in my eyes.

I was so thankful to be holding Johanna in my arms. She was safe and secure and alive. But in that moment, I realized that her newborn weeks were a blur to me. From the moment Johanna was born, my instincts went into a survival mode to protect my baby. In that newborn stage, there were very few sweet moments, at least not for me, as I waited for the rest of the world to see and understand that my baby needed help.

Listening to that newborn baby cry, I realized that those days were truly gone forever. No one could give back that time to me. I had to learn how to grieve the loss in order to restore life.

Grief is a very important piece in the lives of caregivers; it is especially important for parents of children born with disabilities. When you are a parent, it's a very unsettling feeling to experience grief as if you have lost your child while they are standing right in front of you. I felt bad grieving the loss of my newborn while I was holding my infant in my arms. Shouldn't I just be grateful that she is here?

It took me even longer to acknowledge the grief that comes with the birth of a special needs child. The joy of new life is always there because this child is a person created by God. Yet we grieve for what could have been and what might never be.

Grief comes in waves for caregivers. For spouses whose loved ones have become disabled, it's the loss of a life you thought you'd be spending together. The relationship is not over, but it's changed. For children who find themselves in the position of parenting the parent, the role reversal comes with its own kind of grief. The grief of a caregiver is unique compared to other kinds of grief. Yet it is still grief. The loss is sometimes hard to identify because the person you are grieving is right in front of you.

In our case, I look on my daughter Johanna as a living and breathing miracle. Every day is another day of profound grace with its own lessons to learn and life to be lived. However, at different stages of her life, I have grieved the loss of the life I thought she could be living, free of pain.

When she was younger, I grieved that she couldn't walk or ride a bike like other kids. When Johanna turned ten, I realized that she wasn't going to outgrow this disease. It was going to impact the rest of her life and ours. When she turned eighteen, I realized that I no longer have a child with disabilities, but rather a young adult with disabilities who will live with me for the rest of her life. When Johanna talks about getting married and having children, I grieve for her, realizing that marriage and family is probably not in her future. Although she has survived so much, there is still a need to grieve what has been lost.

Grief is a vital part of restoration. It doesn't always mean to replace something or bring it back to its original character. In the caregiver's story, restoration is about grieving the losses and replacing what has been lost with something new and more beautiful.

When we built our home, we chose a distressed look to the walls, floors and furniture. It was an easy choice with four kids, three dogs and three cats. The distressed look was easy. It happened every day. At one point, I remember my son asked my husband and me why we wanted our new house to look so old. We explained that we liked the old farmhouse look. It suits us and it was easier to care for an old house than to keep a new one in perfect condition. Restoring our family was also like that. Our family is far from perfect; indeed we show signs of distress. But that distressed look is becoming a part of who we are now. Restoration doesn't mean we hide the distress; we just find a new kind of beauty and rest in that.

We choose to live in the wine country on the North Fork of Long Island's East End so I can see the sky. It changes throughout the day and is star studded at night. Out here in nature, my soul finds rest and restoration. I believe God intended the beauty of the natural world to help us rest, and to restore our souls. I will never take the North Fork skies for granted. I experience restoration when I look at the ever changing sky. Sometimes, when I wake up in the morning and I see the hint of the pink sunrise coming up on the horizon, I jump out of bed. I take a walk or sit on the front porch, just to appreciate the beautiful sky. It is rest for my mind and my soul.

I also love to sing. I am a seasoned worship leader, a long time Catholic charismatic who loves to lead women into an intimate experience of the Lord in song. I have led small and large groups in song. It's a lot of work, learning new music, running sound and being sensitive to how the congregation is responding. But it is also a place of restoration for me. Praising God and counting my blessings restores my body and my soul. Just the sheer physiology of singing calms my nerves and floods my body with oxygen. Even when I am leading hundreds of people in song, I experience restoration of my mind, body and soul.

Recreation time with family is also a way to restore our bodies from the anxieties of life. But recreation time with a child who has special needs can also be stressful.

I recall a trip to the water park when I had a minor panic attack as I was holding Johanna in a boat on a lazy river ride. She was fussy and trying to jump. I felt my "fight or flight" reactions set in. For a moment I was paralyzed with the thought that my nightmares were becoming reality and this subconscious scenario was going to play out in real life. I feared Johanna would slip through my hands only to drown just outside my grasp.

My husband caught my panicked look from across the wavy river and paddled hard to reach me to take Johanna in his boat. As silly a scene as this seems in reality, the subconscious fear of drowning was powerful.

In truth, the fear ran deeper than drowning. The root fear was losing control. I had to realize that there are circumstances in our lives that are just beyond our control.

God's voice in my sleep changed years of those nightmares into a dream that gave me a vision for a future full of hope. I learned that breathing requires: restoration of my body through sleep and good nutrition, restoration of my soul through prayer, and restoration of my mind through a change of perspective. I also realized that God wastes nothing. Everything can be for our good, and all trials can be restored into blessings, if only we believe.

REFLECT

Right now, you may feel like you are drowning. If restoration means to replace what has been lost, then what do we do when we feel like all our resources have been depleted and there is nothing left?

• Where do you find rest?

• What and who restores you? Can you count your blessings?

Besides restful waters he leads me. He restores my soul.
Psalm 23:2

NOTES

CHAPTER SIX

ENGAGE

In the early days of my daughter's diagnosis, it would have been nice to disconnect from everyone and everything for a very long time. But life with children makes that disconnection difficult, and when one of those children is medically fragile, it's almost impossible. Rather than seeing this as a disadvantage, I have learned to embrace the need to connect and engage to stay alive—to breathe deeply even when the waters rise over my head.

The definition of engage is to occupy, attract or hold someone's attention. Engage also means to participate or become involved in something. Engage is a vitally important strategy for thriving in the trials of life. For me it is as important as believing that God has a plan. Engaging requires connection: with ourselves, our struggles, and others who walk alongside us on the journey.

For the last few years, I have visited a clinic in Chicago with my daughter. It's the only research clinic in the world that studies CCM3, the rare disease that afflicts my daughter. They do a specialized MRI with an evaluation that gives us an expert opinion of her very complicated disease; this also gives the researchers more information towards a cure.

The last time we visited, I coordinated the trip to coincide with meeting a friend from California who was visiting the same clinic. I met my friend Liz online through the Angioma Alliance which is the grass roots organization searching for a cure for cavernous angiomas. She's a really smart lady and I admire her advocacy work and her commitment to her family.

I remember the first time we spoke on the phone. It was as if we had known each other all of our lives. The more we talked, the more we had in common. The first was obvious; Liz and two of her three sons have CCM3. Her sons have struggled with brain hemorrhages and have had brain surgeries as well. Liz is not symptomatic. She gives us all hope!

It was amazing to realize the incredible parallels of our lives. Liz and her family are also devout Catholics with a vibrant faith. Belief is the foundation of their success in dealing with this disease. Liz and I laughed out loud when we shared that we were both homeschooling families as well. Our conversations were more than the details of life. They were opportunities to engage with a kindred spirit and offer one another support along the journey.

Liz and I first met in person two years ago when we hosted a fundraiser for the Angioma Alliance on Long Island. A deep bond was formed. Meeting at the clinic in Chicago gave time for our kids to connect as well as for us to engage in laughter and conversation, sharing this journey and our faith.

After our visits to the clinic, Liz and I met in the dining room of the Ronald McDonald House where both families stayed. There were some good details and some really bad ones as well. Tears glistened in our eyes as we shared the gravity of our situations with one another.

Some of the lesions in our kids' brains were stable; others were hemorrhaging and causing swelling. One of Liz's sons required surgery a few months later. I came away from that appointment very somber, realizing that my daughter is really beyond the scope of being helped by surgical treatments. Johanna's disease has progressed to a point where we have to try to manage the symptoms of hemorrhaging and swelling in the brain as best as we can. But surgery to remove one of these malformations is not really an option unless she is at the point of severe decline. Even then, the risks and benefits have to be strongly considered before anything can be done. If a medical trial opens, Johanna can be considered, but that may still be a long way off.

Although Liz and I have known each other for only about five years, there was no one else in the world that I wanted to share this news with but her—mom to mom. I knew she understood. Even as supportive as my husband and family can be, no one understands the pain of CCM3 like my friend Liz. It is a bond that connects us and makes it easy to engage.

Staying at the Ronald McDonald House near the hospital is a place of profound connection. Families whose children have life-threatening medical issues stay there with their kids to receive outpatient services or to seek respite for themselves while their child is in the hospital. The Ronald McDonald House is a busy place. There are opportunities for families to participate in activities and to share meals. Stories are shared in conversations, in glances and in the journals that are placed in each guest room.

As a writer, I find the journals in the room to be a powerful gift to help me engage with others' stories. These stories offer me the strength of human connections born from these struggles. Families who come to Ronald McDonald Houses to stay have really sick kids. Parents of children with medical issues have a unique understanding of these challenges.

While we stayed there, a young girl I have never met touched my heart. I read her story in the journal on the desk in our room. Her words moved me deeply. When she and her family had stayed at the Ronald McDonald House, she wrote; "I have a lesion in my brain. I have seen a lot of doctors because my legs always hurt and they think it's from the lesion. I have to sit and watch my friends play because it hurts to play and dance."

As I read this little girl's words, I felt her pain. Then, from the pages of the journal, this child touched my heart with the compassion and hope in her words: "If your family is going through tough times, don't be afraid to ask for help and I'll pray for you."

Somehow, I knew she was praying for me and for countless others who walk this lonely journey. Knowing that she's been there helped me to face the days ahead.

During our stay in Chicago, I also had the opportunity to speak to a support group for parents of children with Down Syndrome. While the internet limits some of the depths of our connections with each other to "likes" and status updates, it does provide us with opportunities to engage in conversations with people we might not otherwise meet.

I ended up giving this talk in Chicago because the leader of that group heard me interviewed on a nationally syndicated Catholic radio program. She reached out to me through my website, asking if I would consider speaking to their parent support group.

As God would have it, our visit to Chicago coincided with World Down Syndrome Day. That happened to be the only night I had available to speak. The group celebrated their very special children and that special day with me.

I shared my stories, the joys and the challenges, in the context of the breathing underwater dream. As I shared the 7 strategies with these beautiful parents, using the acronym *B.R.E.A.T.H.E.*, I was uplifted by their laughter and touched by their tears. They each had their own stories to tell how their special children, often misunderstood and rejected, have blessed their lives with deep meaning and purpose. Connecting with others who understand our struggles is an essential key to learning to survive and to breathing underwater.

A natural tendency of a caregiver, indeed anyone under chronic stress, is to disconnect. While healthy disconnects are essential (a strategy I discuss in chapter eight), people who are stressed tend to choose unhealthy options that may lead to addictions. If you Google caregivers and addictions, you will find plenty of research indicating that caregivers are prone to prescription drug and alcohol addictions. I prefer a good heart to heart conversation with my spouse or a friend than a glass of wine or funny white pill any day. The statistics tell me I'm in the minority.

My favorite form of connection, and a great way to disconnect, is my dogs. Over 10 years ago, my daughter received a wonderful service dog through Canine Companions for Independence, a non-profit that places "exceptional dogs with exceptional people"(cci.org).

A year after Johanna received her service dog, Taffy, my then twelve year old MaryAngela begged us to raise puppies for the organization. Nine years and five puppies later, we are glad that we did. These dogs brought their own type of therapeutic connections, even while we were training them.

Our first puppy, a black lab named Lorenz, failed the program and lives with us as a certified therapy dog. We call him the "tempur-pedic" dog because he seeks out the person who is most in need, politely asks permission and then mushes into you with just the right amount of pressure. Endorphins are released which relax the same parts of the brain as drugs and alcohol. What's the moral of the story? Get a dog.

Ten years ago, I experienced a very serious "disconnect" that changed my life forever. My husband and I were doing the music at church for

Palm Sunday Mass. During the liturgy, I began to lose all sensations on the right side of my body. I felt like my face was drooping and my arm and leg became very heavy. It was as if someone had drawn a line down the center of my body. Everything on my right side felt disconnected from the rest of my body. I felt like I was having a stroke.

Given the family history, I went straight to the emergency room and was evaluated for a stroke. Thankfully, it was not a stroke, but it was recommended that I see a neurologist. For the next ten years, I had neurological exams and assessments that confirmed damage in the connections between my brain and sensations on the right side of my body. But the brain scans were inconclusive.

After a few years, better MRI technology revealed one or two demyelinating lesions that could be indicative of Multiple Sclerosis (MS). A few years later, menopausal changes hit and I also contracted Lyme's disease. Those changes activated the right sided symptoms even more. I lose my balance more and forget anything on my right side, especially things I'm holding in my right hand. My right side is frequently bruised because I keep bumping into walls. Most recently, more lesions occurred which correlated with these clinical symptoms, and I was diagnosed with multiple sclerosis.

Rather than seeing MS as a death sentence, I see it as an opportunity to set clear boundaries in my life. The disconnection between my brain and my body teaches me that I need to engage my senses and pay closer attention to my own needs for self-care. I fatigue easily and I need a lot of sleep. I also need to take medications to be sure the disease remains on a slow progression.

Connecting with others, myself and God for support helps me believe that the dark ocean of these trials is mercy in disguise. I have learned that we are never alone in our struggles. When we feel stress and tribulations mounting above our heads like the rising tide, we are but one breath away from finding new life and new hope.

Sometimes, it hurts to engage. But we have to engage if we are to survive and thrive in our difficult circumstances.

REFLECT

Choose a friend you trust with your deepest pain, someone who can handle the grief and help you connect. Seeking out a coach, a therapist to help end an addiction, or a support group to help you connect with others, are all ways to help you breathe.

Go outside and engage your senses. Feel the pain, hand it over to God and just breathe.

• Where are you feeling disconnected?

• How can you begin to engage with yourself, others and God?

Dismiss anxiety, surrender to God with petitions full of gratitude.
Philippians 4:6

NOTES

CHAPTER SEVEN

ADVOCATE

When I was in college, I learned to fly, not literally of course, but on a plane. Home was a ten-hour drive, and sometimes it was just easier for my parents to fly me home. Often it was even cheaper, especially with the advent of discount fares on no-frill airlines.

I loved flying. I loved looking out the window. I loved watching all the people boarding and wondering where they were going. I was on my own, by myself with no one else to look after. I paid attention to the pre-flight instructions on those first trips, but after a few flights, I just tuned them out, figuring that my life was in God's hands anyway. What did it matter?

When I became a mother, it mattered a lot. So did a lot of other things. Something clicks in you when you have a baby and you realize that another human being is totally dependent on you for survival. I started to pay attention to a lot of things that didn't matter before I had children. Suddenly I cared about myself and the world around me much more because my kids needed me. I wanted them to live happy, holy and purposeful lives, and I wanted to be there to share it with them.

When I became a mom, I started to develop a little anxiety about flying. We didn't do much flying, but because we lived on the East Coast and my husband's family is from the Midwest, we flew at least once a year. Flying is so much more stressful with kids. You worry about the changes in pressure, the distractions and the lack of mobility (especially for a toddler).

Suddenly, I found myself paying very close attention to the pre-flight instructions. I memorized the wing exits, made sure the seatbelts were securely fastened, and even read up on what to do in the unlikely event of a water landing. But the oxygen mask was a challenge for me. It went against my nature to consider this concept of putting myself first. I studied the advice and wondered if mothers were consulted when the airlines wrote up the pre-flight instruction manuals. I thought, "How can I put the oxygen mask on myself before I put it on my child? There must be something wrong with this advice."

Four children—one of them with very special needs—validated the airlines' research. I didn't need to read much further; I found it out on my own the first time I had a hard time breathing. This simple pre-flight instruction card that I had flatly ignored as a single woman became a metaphor for surviving life with kids. It became critical to me when Johanna was born.

I realized that I had to put the oxygen mask on myself first if I was going to help her and our family continue to breathe. In other words, I couldn't advocate for my family's needs and most especially for Johanna unless I first advocated for myself and took care of my needs. You can't help someone if you are unconscious.

I became an advocate when I became a mother. The first time someone challenged my parenting skills and style when my son was three weeks old, I discovered my inner lioness. My lioness was protective and strong, always on guard and ready to pounce on predators who threatened her children. Being somewhat of a quiet person, I didn't realize that I could be so strong. Motherhood changed all that.

To a certain degree, the skills of advocacy I learned with my three older children helped to season me and give me the confidence that I needed to be Johanna's mother. But nothing quite prepared me to advocate for a child with medical issues like Johanna's.

My skills were challenged the very first day when I knew Johanna and I needed to continue breastfeeding. I had to quickly learn that although I was technically out of my environment in the frightening world of hospitals and healthcare, I still knew my baby better than anyone. So, by the time Johanna was ten months old and had had six brain surgeries, the nurses in the PICU knew the drill. When they saw Johanna's name pop up on the roster, they exchanged the crib for a patient bed, padded the side rails, and made sure that everyone knew mom and baby slept best side by side with nursing on demand.

I refined my lioness traits to seek out answers for things I didn't understand and learned to speak a whole new language with confidence and grace. When I didn't understand what was happening, I asked questions and did research online. I studied neurological journals and read everything I could on the diseases that affected Johanna.

Mothering Johanna taught me advocacy skills that I never knew I had, not the least of which was how to get a hot shower and put on make-up before the doctors made their rounds. Truly, when I coach caregivers, most especially moms, I tell them that one of the most beneficial things you can do to advocate for your loved one it is to take a shower and get dressed. Initially they think I'm crazy, but deep inside, they know I'm right.

In the early days of Johanna's diagnosis, I was at a serious disadvantage. Not only was I stuck in the PICU with a critically ill baby, but I was also postpartum. I still had baby fat, so sweat pants were my best friends. No one expected me to dress the part of the all-together mom when my baby was having brain surgery. No one even suggested that, except an older and wiser lioness. She had been walking this journey a few steps ahead of me.

Moms connect with moms pretty easily when their kids have something in common. Being in the PICU is just the same as being at the playground, only not. The stakes are much higher than teaching your kids to share their toys. I've met some pretty amazing mothers through the years who have all contributed to the mother I am today. The mom who taught me the benefits of taking a shower and putting on make-up helped lay a strong foundation for advocacy.

When we spoke, she shared the years of her journey and the number of surgeries her son had undergone. We compared notes on doctors, diagnoses, and on managing families and careers with a medically fragile child. I noticed how pretty she looked. She was always nicely dressed, thoughtful, articulate, and she always wore make-up and had shoes on. I was frumpy. My hair was gathered in a bun, and I preferred to wear slippers until I had to go outside the hospital.

The coolest thing about this mom was that I didn't feel any condemnation for my looks despite her neat appearance. She understood my situation and state of mind and never said anything about my appearance. When I commented on how she looked so warm and wonderful even though she had been walking this journey for so many years, she gently shared her wisdom with me.

This mom smiled at me, and then she gently took me under her wings. She asked me how I would feel about taking medical advice from a doctor who wore sweats, with bed-head hair, obviously needing a shower. With her kind words and gentle example, I realized how taking better care of myself would also empower my ability to advocate for my daughter.

For years now, whenever we are in the hospital, I get up very early to shower, dress and put on make-up and shoes! By the time the doctors make their rounds, I am ready to listen and share my concerns for my daughter's health. I have seen how much better the doctors and nurses respond to our needs when I look professional and am confident about my appearance. If it's a particularly long and difficult hospitalization, I even wear my heels.

Other simple ways that I advocate for my daughter include keeping an online record of surgeries, a file of doctor's numbers, and copies of reports and scans. I also keep educational records and stay abreast of special education laws to ensure Johanna receives a free and appropriate education.

I learned to Google terms and research topics that I didn't understand so that I could confidently be an integral part of the conversation and make intelligent and informed healthcare decisions in regards to her care.

I also learned to trust my gut instinct. Over the years, those instincts have been refined with knowledge and experience to develop what my husband calls "Mom's Radical Instinct" or the "MOMRI." World renowned neurosurgeons and other doctors have commented to me that my instincts and understanding regarding the neurological conditions affecting Johanna are impressive and valuable. Developing this instinct and knowledge took hard work and a lot of time, but in the end it paid off in advocating for Johanna.

When we started this journey over eighteen years ago, I could not have imagined that advocating for my needs as a caregiver and my daughter's needs as a person with disabilities would lead us into a national conversation on healthcare.

Years ago, just as the Affordable Care Act (ACA) was proposed, I was asked to participate in a press conference in front of the Capital in Washington, D.C. Johanna and I, with her service dog Taffy, joined other parents of kids with special needs to share our concerns regarding federalized healthcare and regulations that could discriminate against the needs of the unborn, the disabled and the elderly. On this little field trip to Washington, D.C., I recognized that I had a gift for advocacy on a larger scale.

In 2008, my husband's career in church ministry ended as parishes and dioceses around the country downsized to deal with diminishing collections due to an unstable economy. When people are fearful about money, they stop supporting non-profit work—including churches.

We sporadically collected unemployment as we struggled to rebuild our lives as entrepreneurs and to pay our bills. We had to insure our family with a medically fragile child for whom the insurance company pays out over $150K annually. It was, and still is, a daunting task. Hospital bills and costs of daily living mounted and we found ourselves sinking deeper into debt and unable to pay our mortgage. After a few months, we went bankrupt and our home went into foreclosure.

We tried negotiating with the bank to modify our loan. My husband worked day and night tracking and submitting paperwork the bank needed—all the while looking for a new job with benefits and building our home business. Our income grew primarily through his diligence and hard work, with me doing some writing and wellness coaching on the side. We were both learning new skills as entrepreneurs, but we felt like criminals in our own home. Somehow, our lovely home on the North Fork, our house that love built, was slipping through our fingers, being washed away with the housing market crash. Those were two of the most difficult years of our entire married life.

After dotting each "i" and crossing every "t," showing increased income to support a mortgage, our loan modification was finally denied. We got the letter the day after Thanksgiving. We were devastated.

During this whole time, people had been encouraging me to use my advocacy and writing skills to tell our story to the public and to see if we could get help securing a loan. My husband resisted because he felt that it would have a negative impact on our business. I wrote the story in my heart and head, ready to be released at the proper time.

A week after Thanksgiving and after the denial from the bank, we learned that Johanna developed another type of brain tumor that seemed unrelated to the multiple cavernous angiomas already in her brain. We were prepared for the possibility that it could be cancerous, possibly caused by the amount of CT scans and x-rays she had over the years.

There was more testing to be done before we could plan this brain surgery. In the midst of scheduling the surgery, we were getting letters from the bank telling us our house would be foreclosed on in January. When I was on the phone with the neurosurgeons office, trying to schedule Johanna's surgery with time for her to recuperate before we needed to move, I lost it. I realized then and there that I had to use every gift of advocacy I had to save our home, and it had to be done now. So I picked up my laptop and wrote an article.

Our story was like many other Americans who also lost jobs and trudged through long loan modification processes while incurring more debt and facing frightening deadlines as they worked to secure a future in their home. But ours differed because we had the added incentive and extenuating circumstances of Johanna's medical needs.

A local paper agreed to publish our story after Christmas in hopes of getting it to some major news outlets. A generous lawyer heard about our case through friends and offered to advocate for us for free. She also sent my article to other connections. Somehow, we still don't exactly know how, it made it into the hands of an executive from the bank that held our mortgage.

That Christmas Eve, as we were just about ready to leave for Mass, my cell phone rang and it was our bank. The bank didn't have my cell number on our mortgage or modification documents; they only had my husband's. We specifically omitted mine so I didn't have to take their calls. However, all my contact information was in the article. I hesitated to answer because we were leaving for church. But I am very glad that I did.

The man on the other end of the line introduced himself as being from Wells Fargo Bank. He said, "I'm calling to tell you that the bank has decided to hand-write your loan modification and to wish your family a very, Merry Christmas!"

I was in shock. I asked him to repeat everything so that I could write down the information of the names and numbers we needed. He promised that the bank would be in touch in the New Year and that the new terms of our mortgage would be arriving by certified mail. I thanked him profusely—through my tears.

By the time I went downstairs to the kitchen where my family was waiting to go to church, I was hysterically crying. My husband thought that someone had died, and my children feared the worst. Instead, as I managed to get the story out, my family cheered and embraced each other with sobs of joy! It was truly like the Christmas Eve scene from "It's a Wonderful Life!" There was much gratitude in our hearts that Christmas. Advocacy and prayer saved the house that love built to continue on into a future of hope.

The next hurdle was continuing to ensure that we could weather the changes in the Affordable Care Act. After the ACA was passed, I was concerned about what was going to happen to our health insurance—how we were personally going to be affected.

Other people had time to shop around and deal with the bureaucratic backlog; we didn't have that luxury. We now purchased our health insurance on our own as a small business. It was small businesses who took the first hit in the disastrous rollout of the ACA in the fall of 2013. I trusted in the Lord to care for our needs, but I knew that time and again, the Lord used us to ensure a future for our children, especially for Johanna.

While President Obama promised, in his infamous statements, "If you like your doctor, you can keep your doctor. If you like your health insurance plan, you can keep your plan," I had my doubts. It just didn't make sense to me. The math didn't add up.

During the ACA rollout, as I sat at my daughter's bedside, I confirmed with our health insurance company that our plan was being terminated due to Obamacare. They told me that the termination letter should reach me any day. I thanked the woman on the phone who said that she had spoken to countless numbers of people that day who were facing the same predicament. I wondered how many of them were sitting next to their child who had just had her 85th surgery.

Through my tears, I briefly explained my dilemma and left a nurse to care for my daughter while I stepped out to call my husband. We brainstormed scenarios, but it was all terribly frightening from so many angles. Finally, I told my husband that I really felt that we needed to bring our situation to another level of advocacy, both to help ourselves and to help shed light for the thousands of others whose insurance plans were being terminated.

I had been a long time viewer and listener of conservative television and radio talk show host, Sean Hannity. Sean is a fierce advocate of Constitutional rights for every American. He asks hard questions that are not readily posed in main stream media.

Faced with an impending termination, I decided it was time to bring our story into the national news. My husband agreed. The following morning, I sent an email to the Associate Producer at the Hannity radio show. The next day Johanna was released from the hospital. On the way home, I called the talk show repeatedly on the three hour drive on the Long Island Expressway (LIE). The LIE runs from the Queens Midtown Tunnel in Manhattan all the way out to the East End of Long Island in Riverhead, NY.

When I finally reached the end of the LIE, the radio show ended and the Associate Producer answered my call. We spoke at length about our situation as she read my email and asked me detailed questions. My persistence and advocacy skills opened the door to a national conversation on how Obamacare affected our family.

In the coming weeks, I worked with this wonderful woman to gather paperwork and articulate the details of our story for a segment on the radio program. I recommended that our pediatrician, Dr. Roberta Nataloni, also be interviewed on the program. She has been our pediatrician for over 20 years, and she has taught me so much about advocating for my children's health and standing for life issues.

In addition to pursuing medicine, Dr. Nataloni is a student of history, and she immigrated to the United States from Italy. Her knowledge of history and her personal life experience have made her a strong defender of constitutional freedom and the right to life for every human being from conception to natural death. I looked to Dr. Nataloni to understand the Affordable Care Act and its effects on healthcare and the Constitutional rights of Americans. Her wisdom as a pediatrician and an advocate has been invaluable.

The Sean Hannity Show decided to interview both of us on the nationally syndicated radio program. After a week of emails back and forth and conversations on the phone, we were scheduled for a Friday afternoon. I set myself up in my writing room in our barn in the backyard. I gathered my notes and my Bible and practiced some deep breathing so I wouldn't throw up.

As frightening as this new adventure appeared, I knew it was the right thing to do. I knew that our story would help shed light on issues facing many Americans, especially those who were medically fragile and disabled. Five minutes before the interview was scheduled, the producer called me. As we talked, she asked me where I was, explaining that every other time we talked it sounded fine, but today there were too many echoes. I panicked and explained to her that I had set up in the barn. She asked me to quickly move back into my house and call her back. I ran back into my house and closed myself off in my bedroom to take the remaining two minutes to catch my breath. So much for being relaxed and prepared!

The interview went very well. Dr. Nataloni and I had ample time to express our concerns over the ACA and add some constructive ideas to the conversation. The news traveled all over the United States. My young adult children were contacted by college friends from across the country asking about our family. People contacted me on Facebook, and other news outlets picked up our story, which was an extreme example of the negative impacts of the ACA. It helped to fuel a national debate towards better solutions. They repeated the program again the day after Thanksgiving. At the end of the year, the Sean Hannity Show listed our interview online in their "Best of 2013" segments.

Shortly after the radio interview, other news outlets contacted me. The Heritage Foundation wrote an article that was also picked up on LifeSite News. I write a weekly spiritual reflection column entitled "Life on Purpose" for our hyper-local news site, RiverheadLocal.com, and they carried an excellent piece which was linked on news sites throughout the country.

In the midst of the debate, I had to get to work to secure insurance for our family. I began the arduous task of making phone calls to insurance companies and waiting on hold for hours. I also began calling our New York State agencies to see if the reimbursement programs that had been available to us before the ACA were still going to be there. What I found was, despite the fact that this was four years in the making, no one knew what to expect or how to implement the changes. The only thing that was certain was that our monthly premiums were going up by $1000.

A week later, Fox News called me and arranged for me to appear on the Hannity television program. In the midst of this, Johanna got very sick and was admitted to the PICU at New York University Hospital (NYU) for the sixth time that year. She underwent numerous procedures and shunt revisions. It was very difficult to be researching insurance companies and doing this advocacy work while I was caring for Johanna in the hospital. Still, every morning when I awoke at 5 a.m. to shower before doctor rounds, I knew that my work as a mother and an advocate was life changing for Johanna and for the millions of Americans who faced similar situations.

The television interview was scheduled for the first Friday in December. We were still in NYU hospital, so Fox News arranged to send a car. My eldest daughter picked out an outfit for me to wear. I bought new black pumps. It was a strange experience to shower and dress up for an appearance on national television while waiting in the PICU. It was that very experience that motivated me to advocate for our needs.

Thankfully, Johanna was discharged in time to go with me to the studio. The drive to Fox News was surreal. My husband, my two daughters and Johanna's CCI service dog, Taffy, climbed into the limo as we made our way uptown to Fox News Headquarters. It was a beautiful way to see the sparkling lights of the city. Rockefeller Center's Christmas tree had just been lit. Christmas time is the best time in New York City. I felt like we were living characters on the pages of a children's book. I am willing to do whatever it takes to advocate for my little girl, even if it means going to the White House.

The best part of the interview was meeting everyone in the green room. Sean Hannity is the real deal. There were no airs and no bodyguards, just real people doing the work of real news. Sean was genuinely impressive, not because of his personality or his knowledge or the people he knows in high places. Johanna, just out of another brain surgery, sat in her wheelchair, excited but weary. Sean saw that and simply sat on the floor at her feet. He asked her lots of questions about life and her really cool service dog, Taffy. He encouraged her by sharing how much he was inspired by people like her who struggle but don't give up. There were no cameras or photographers (though they did have great beauticians, and I was very glad for that), just real people who cared enough to tell our story.

During the interview, I was nervous but inspired. There was a great peace that filled my heart and soul and gave me clarity of mind. My family sat in the studio and watched. Out of the corner of my eye, I could see them in the shadows. It helped to keep me focused on my "why" for this moment. Sean, an excellent interviewer, helped me get my points across and tell our story. I shared my concerns about the ACA and how I thought things needed to be different. We highlighted the lack of transparency in the passage of the law and the misleading information purported from President Obama himself who promised that if I liked my plan and my doctors, I could keep them. In the end, that was not true.

After the interview was over, I just wanted to run home, cuddle Johanna in my arms, and make the world go away. People from across the nation began to contact me through Facebook with promises of prayers; they also thanked me for standing up for others who faced a similar plight.

I worked diligently over the next three months. What I witnessed in the insurance industry and in the healthcare system was akin to a natural disaster. Every agency I contacted, every insurance company, doctor's office and hospital, the answers were still the same; chaos reigned in America's healthcare. Doctors were finding out that they weren't included in plans. Plans were revealing massive premium hikes and high deductibles. People had to drive hours for specialists because of mandates in their plans.

After months of massive research, I made a wrong decision based on money. I opted for the cheapest plan with a $1500 a month premium (crazy). It mirrored one of the federal exchange plans, but promised that it did not come with the same problems. Again, I was misled— along with millions of other Americans. During the one month that we had that plan, Johanna's skin broke down and a recent incision opened to reveal her skull. She required hospital isolation for two staph infections, reconstructive surgery, IV infusions of round the clock antibiotic therapy for 40 days and a host of other interventions. Eight months later, I am still dealing with the lack of coverage that "affordable plan" cost me.

Just prior to that time, I was in the PICU with Johanna for a long and grueling stay. She was very sick with a serious shunt malfunction and required three brain surgeries in three weeks.

During that hospital stay, Senate Majority leader, Senator Harry Reid, made a speech from the Senate Floor that infuriated me even more than the ACA itself. On every American's dime, Senator Reid read a prepared and calculated speech in which he said that all of us who were telling stories of Obamacare struggles were liars. He said the stories were all lies promulgated by the Republicans for political gain. Senator Reid, one of my public servants in the US Senate, called me a liar from the Senate Floor! I was livid when I watched the video.

The lioness in me, three weeks of sleep deprivation, and access to social media combined and became the perfect storm to unleash my opinions. I posted the video to Facebook and made the following comment: "Dear Senator Reid, I dare you to come to the Pediatric ICU at NYU Langone in New York City and say these words to my face!"

Senator Reid must not have been on Facebook that day, but apparently Fox News was because within five minutes, I got a phone call from one of the producers of Fox & Friends asking me if I would like to appear on the show the next morning to respond to Senator Reid's comments on the national news! I was a little taken aback and jokingly asked if they were stalking me. They said it was a coincidence.

I told the producer that as much as I would like to respond, I had to see what would happen with my daughter. There was a slight chance that she would be scheduled for brain surgery that next morning when Fox wanted to interview me. Within the next hour, a strange set of circumstances occurred, and our neurosurgeon told me that he was taking Johanna to surgery that same afternoon. The possibility existed that I could do the interview.

I called the producer back and told her what was happening. I explained that I would agree to the interview only if I had a number that I could call and cancel any time prior to their car picking me up. The surgery should go well and I would have world-class nurses and doctors caring for my daughter. But still, if my little girl needed me, I just couldn't be there for the interview. They agreed and gave me the contact number, and we left it at that.

The surgery did go well, and Johanna slept peacefully during that night. As I sat in the recliner beside her bed, I realized that the date of the interview, February 28th, was Rare Disease Day. All over Facebook, people whose lives were affected by rare disease posted logos and signs indicating that someone they loved had a rare disease. It was a day set aside to increase awareness and advocacy for those we love. I recognized that I had a rare opportunity to highlight CCM3 and send a message to our leaders in Washington, especially Senator Harry Reid, that they are employed by American people and we demand greater respect.

Unlike the Hannity show, I had no time to plan for an outfit. I had been in the hospital for three weeks, so I could only choose the best I had out of my suitcase and go. I was so glad for their hairstylists and make-up artists! I wish I could visit them once a week! The car picked me up before the sun rose on the cold February morning.

Elisabeth Hasselbeck was the interviewer that morning on Fox and Friends. She replayed the clip of Senator Reid's speech and then we talked. Elisabeth was warm and compassionate as she helped me articulate what was on my heart. I explained that prior to Obamacare, we had health insurance that covered the majority of our hospital visit to the University of Chicago's CCM3 clinic, the only one in the world. But since Obamacare, we have no out of state coverage, and the Angioma Alliance would be paying the bill.

That morning on national television, I asked the Senate Majority Leader to apologize to the American people. I challenged him requesting that in honor of Rare Disease Day he put his money where his mouth is and make a $30k donation to the Angioma Alliance in honor of my daughter, to pay for her visit to the CCM3 clinic.

Elisabeth Hasselbeck affirmed me saying, "Eileen Benthal, I don't know what you're made of, but I like it."

Senator Reid never did make that donation. Rush Limbaugh carried the interview on his radio program as well. As I rode back to NYU in the car Fox News provided, people from all over the country again were messaging me on Facebook. They were thanking me for giving them a voice in this national debate. They were grateful that I stood up and demanded respect from a high ranking official in the United States government. I was deeply moved by the flood of impassioned responses.

I snuck back into Johanna's room before her breakfast tray arrived and before the doctors made their morning rounds. No one knew except the nurse in charge of Johanna. My little girl smiled at me, knowing where I was and what I was doing. I told her that someday she and I were going to Washington. I would give a speech from the Senate floor to remind the politicians who they work for and why they should care. Johanna, recovering well from her 89th surgery, gave me a big smile, with her thumbs up. That was the best part of my day, and it's all that really mattered.

REFLECT

Each one of us has what it takes to stand up for ourselves, our loved ones and those who need us the most. Discover your passion and define your purpose—you will find your voice to advocate.

• What matters to you?

• How do you best advocate for yourself and your loved ones?

If the Lord was not with us, the flood would have engulfed us, the torrent would have swept over us and the raging waters would have swept us away.

Psalm 124:2, 4-5

NOTES

CHAPTER EIGHT

TIME

The biggest change in my life since Johanna's birth is my perspective on time. There is nothing quite like facing the mortality of your own child to make you realize that time is a gift and it is certainly not your own.

I remember the long drive from the doctor's office to the emergency room that beautiful autumn day in the middle of November when Johanna was first diagnosed. I had the distinct impression that heaven and earth were somehow converging, at least in my mind, for that endless fifteen minute drive. It was like a movie on fast forward. I had an overwhelming sense that a "heavenly cloud of witnesses" (Hebrews 12) was praying for Johanna and me and for our whole family. Emerging from this fast forwarded video, I heard a tiny voice say, "Mom, I'm praying for you and Johanna. It's going to be all right."

I immediately recognized the voice although I had never heard it before. Before my ramblings confuse you, I don't seek out the dead, but rather as a Catholic Christian, I stand with scripture and church teaching that clearly states that we are surrounded by a heavenly cloud of witnesses. Somehow, in that brief moment, the Lord allowed me to know that a baby I had lost, whom I named Joseph, was praying for us in this dire time.

Time stood still as I briefly recalled the fleeting nine weeks that baby had spent in my womb. I became pregnant when my eldest daughter was just sixteen months old. How I came to love that baby in the short time I knew him, only God knows. But I grieved his passing as if he had moved from my womb to my arms.

Now, five years past the miscarriage, that same sense of maternal loss came over me again. Through that momentary sense of grief, this little voice reminded me again of the maternal, eternal lesson that God brings new life in the midst of every death. I could only hope this transparency of heaven was not a sign that I would again experience the depths of maternal grief by losing my baby Johanna.

Children take time. Some would say they rob us of the little time we have to ourselves. I would say they show us the value of time and teach us as the Psalmist writes, "to number our days aright." Johanna has done that since the day she was born.

I never worried about setting my babies on a schedule. I just got to know who they were and what they needed to grow. Then I figured out how we were going to make this work together. Right from the beginning, we practiced attachment style parenting. I had to laugh that a parenting style had a name. We didn't know or really care about the name. We just knew our babies, did what we felt was right, and lived life from there.

I remember when Johanna was six months old; therapists started coming into our home as part of early intervention. One of the physical therapists remarked that she might have been concerned had Johanna been my first baby. But being held so much by the five of us, this therapist assured us that Johanna's brain would heal from the trauma of those first brain surgeries.

Early on, one neurologist remarked on how I wore Johanna on my body in a baby sling. I told him that it seemed like when she was out of

CHAPTER NINE

HOPE

Hope is another essential strategy to breathing underwater, and it is also the most misunderstood. For most of us, we only dare to hope if we have an indication that our desired outcomes will be reached. We have to have an inkling that what we desire can be attained or we don't hope. When we feel like we are drowning in our circumstances, that kind of circumstantial hope is impossible.

The subtitle of this book "A Caregiver's Journey of Hope" is my manifesto. For over eighteen years now, I have been walking a journey of hope. It sounds kind of like a warm, fuzzy, light kind of thing, doesn't it? But it isn't. Hope only comes in the dark. One of my favorite scriptures on hope says,

> But hope that is seen is no hope at all. Who hopes for what they already have?
>
> Romans 8:24

That says it all. One experience stands out among the rest as the time that I came to really understand hope and how I desperately needed it to keep breathing.

One Thanksgiving, we planned to fly from Long Island to Illinois to celebrate with my husband's family. Johanna had just had another shunt revision. She was released from the hospital just days before we planned to leave. Our neurosurgeon cleared her to fly with us thinking that she would be safe with a newly revised shunt system.

Now all we had to do was pack. With Johanna, packing means emergency medical numbers, medical history and most recent scans of her brain and shunt system. As we packed, an intense foreboding feeling came over me. I was really concerned that things were not going to go well. I tried to ignore the feeling but it just wouldn't go away.

After an uneventful flight, we settled in with family and excitedly greeted relatives we hadn't seen in a few years. Amidst the many preparations for Thanksgiving, I struggled with that foreboding feeling that pressed in on me. It was like a suffocating heat, threatening to shatter our family plans. Just two days into our stay, Johanna's shunt malfunctioned. The pressure began building up in her brain as cerebral spinal fluid leaked out of one of the new incisions.

Family members gave me lots of suggestions of hospitals that we could go to and doctors that we could see. The CCM3 clinic in Chicago had not been developed yet, and we did not have any great local contacts in the area. Even though our neurosurgeon had a doctor that he knew at a hospital in Chicago, we all felt it was safest to fly home to New York.

My husband and I agonized with the decision to have him stay with our older children while I returned home with Johanna. As hard as it was to part, we knew that the kids did not need to spend another holiday in the hospital. We kissed tearful goodbyes as Johanna and I boarded the plane home. The kids stayed with my husband and his family.

Despite the fact that it was the day before Thanksgiving, Southwest Airlines accommodated us at no additional cost. The flight attendants were very helpful. After I explained our situation, I was escorted to the bulk head seating so that Johanna could remain in a reclined position as much as possible. While we were on the plane, I needed to do sterile dressing changes of the wound that was leaking cerebral spinal fluid. The flight was packed, so a young woman sat down next to us.

I told her that I would have to be doing these medical tasks in flight. The young woman smiled in between her tears and told me how she had just said goodbye to her mother who was dying of cancer. She explained that she might not see her mother again. But she vowed to make a difference. This young woman was more than happy to help me entertain Johanna and keep her comfortable on this awkward flight. Johanna rested peacefully in my arms and stared at me with her beautiful blue eyes. There was such wisdom in her eyes, even for a little girl.

After we arrived at the hospital, Johanna had surgery to relieve the pressure and they treated her brain for infection. As Johanna always does, she found the good in the situation and we planned our Thanksgiving Day with our hospital friends. Johanna spoke to my husband and her siblings, laughing at stories and blowing kisses into the phone. My husband and I shared whispers and tried to imagine the warmth of our embrace as we each faced these cold autumn days apart.

We spent a sweet Thanksgiving in the hospital, enjoying a feast with other families. But in the middle of that night Johanna's conditioned worsened. She took an unexpected turn to a neurological decline as the pressure built up in her brain. As her heart rate and respirations plunged, she was placed on a respirator to keep her alive. Then she was rushed back to the operating room for emergency surgery to correct the pressure in her brain. I called my husband and cried.

In the waiting room, I was surrounded by friends who sought to comfort me and pray. I felt like I was in two places at once: my body was in the waiting room, but my spirit and my thoughts were with Johanna in the operating room. All at once, I had a picture in my mind of Johanna, the operating room and her surgeon's hands. I knew something was going terribly wrong. I felt that I was in that operating room praying for Johanna's life and her neurosurgeon. I knew that a move of God was going to take place.

Minutes later, though it felt like hours, Johanna's surgeon came to see me. Our eyes met from a distance, and we both knew something had happened. He carefully explained that Johanna had a catastrophic event, a hemorrhage of a major artery of the brain. He thought we had lost her on the operating room table. But miraculously, the bleeding stopped by itself and her vitals remained stable. While he did not know for certain the brain damage this would cause, at least we knew that the bleeding stopped and Johanna was alive. He explained that he needed to place her in a drug-induced coma to give her brain time to heal.

I sobbed as he talked. By that time, Johanna's godmother had joined me in the waiting room, and we held hands as we listened intently to his explanations. Then I asked Johanna's neurosurgeon if we could pray together, something we had done and shared a few times before. As I prayed aloud, the words flowed like a melody from my soul. It was a bittersweet song, mixed with gratitude for miracles discovered and moaning for pain deeply felt. Where was God? He was right there with us, where two or more gathered in His Name. The path of miracles had taken a new turn, and I wasn't certain where it would lead us.

My very next thought was for my husband and children. I needed to expedite their flight home quickly. We were in a critical time and it was unclear whether Johanna's brain could handle the damage of an arterial bleed. I found myself praying for Johanna to survive long enough to say goodbye to our family. Miraculously, we were able to get them on a plane within hours. When they did arrive that evening, Johanna was in a deep coma. Her icy hands were limp. When I opened her eyelids, cold blue eyes stared off in the distance. It was hard to believe she was alive. What else could I do but hope?

The faith of my other three children amazed me. My then fifteen-year-old son knelt by Johanna's ear, held her icy hand and sang her a lullaby. My daughters, twelve and nine at the time, both chattered lovingly toward Johanna, telling her of their trip from Illinois and all the coming plans for Christmas. Later, they all broke down in my arms. My husband stood quietly by Johanna's bedside and kissed his sweet daughter's head. Single tears rolled down his cheeks but his pained expression did not change. We began our Advent waiting for the Lord to come.

In the weeks to follow, there was little to do but wait. Friends kept our children busy with preparations for Christmas and frequent visits to the hospital. During the few visits I made home for a couple of hours, I felt like I was having out of body experiences. I felt disconnected from the hustle and bustle of the world preparing for the holidays. I remember one day visiting my children at my friend's home. After playing with my kids I went upstairs to take a nap. I never slept. I just sobbed, long, uncontrollable sobs. It felt like my grief would swallow me whole. I longed to return to the solace of Johanna's bedside.

In Johanna's hospital room, we played soft music and lit an artificial Christmas tree. The rhythmic sound of the respirator reminded us that Johanna's life breathed on. Somehow I knew she was in a holy place in between heaven and earth. She was definitely still alive, but not really with us. Right there in her hospital bed, I could feel the presence of God. As stressful as that time was, when I was lying next to Johanna's bed, I felt a deep sense of peace. We set up a tiny manger beside Johanna's bed. As I gazed on the Holy Family in the manger, I knew that Jesus and Mary held Johanna in their hands while we waited.

Those days were tenuous as the pressure in her brain climbed to dangerous limits and an aneurysm developed at the site of the arterial bleed. There were a few emergency surgeries in the middle of the night to clear catheters, running from her brain, that were clogged with blood and debris. After CT scan images showed a growing aneurysm, the doctors decided to wake her gradually to see what lie ahead. Slowly they turned the respirator down, trying to get Johanna to learn to breathe over the tube, on her own once again.

The day they planned to wake Johanna and remove the breathing tube, I felt like I couldn't breathe on my own. I feared that she wouldn't be able to either. I watched her struggle to breathe as the doctors were cautiously encouraging her. They had everything set up and ready to re-intubate her if necessary. They were prepared to put her back on the respirator if she couldn't yet breathe on her own. I felt my knees weaken as I stepped away. Then, prompted by the Spirit, I called out, "Johanna, breathe!"

She turned her falling head toward me, and for the first time in weeks, her dazed blue eyes met mine. And in that moment she took a deep breath that filled both her lungs and mine. I'll never take breathing for granted again.

The next day, as Johanna remembered how to breathe on her own, we prepared for yet another very dangerous surgery. The aneurysm in her artery was growing larger each day. If that aneurysm were to explode, she would most likely die. The week before Christmas, we were transferred to New York City for an extremely complex surgery to close off the blood flow to the aneurysm.

I remember the day of that surgery very well. It was my birthday. Our friends, doctors, nurses and staff, back at the hospital on Long Island, faxed me birthday wishes with promises of prayers for Johanna. The neurosurgeon called us into the operating room to show how large the aneurysm was on the angiogram. Johanna was sleeping on the table with lines coming out of her brain and her groin. He told us that it was a very high risk procedure. He said that he would do his absolute best as a surgeon, but he needed us to do our best in prayer. We left the room confident in his abilities and in the power of prayer. As the surgeon coiled the aneurysm, we prayed.

As we waited, I thought of how I always prayed for snow on my birthday when I was a child. Now I prayed for the Lord to save my daughter. I experienced a strange contrast that gave me hope. During the weeks Johanna was in the coma, I felt like she connected us to eternity, and I knew that heaven was indeed our promised home. I was completely at peace, knowing that on my birthday, Johanna would come home. Either God would place her in my arms or take her to heaven. Either way she was home in the arms of the Lord. That was the greatest birthday gift to me.

God saw fit to place Johanna back in my arms and home to stay with the family who loves her. The recovery, learning to speak and walk and interact again, was slow and precious. We came home from the hospital a few days after Christmas, just in time to celebrate Little Christmas and rejoice in Epiphany, a word that means "a manifestation of God."

People often assume that I ask God why my daughter and my family have to suffer so much. Honestly, it's not a question I ask very often. I choose to believe that the Lord uses all things for good (Romans 8:28). A lot of good has come from that rough season. Our family, though worn out from the struggle, was made stronger. Our children are wiser because they have seen God's power in the midst of suffering. Johanna's neurosurgeon was baptized a Catholic Christian, just eighteen months after that little miracle on the operating room table. He says he couldn't take credit for saving Johanna. God did it.

I learned a lot about hope in that seemingly hopeless situation. If I put my hope in the situation that surrounded us, I would have curled up and died. But hope doesn't need to see; in fact it can't see. In Paul's letter to the Romans he writes:

We hope for what we do not yet have, we wait for it patiently.
Romans 8:22-25

If we could see that everything was going to be fine, that Johanna would live and make a full recovery, we would not need the virtue of hope. Hope is essential. If belief is the mechanism by which we breathe underwater, then hope is the power. Hope is the power of the powerless and the light in the darkness. It does not require that our circumstances change. It only requires us to imagine—that which is impossible is really possible.

REFLECT

If you are waiting for your circumstances to change from hopeless to hopeful, then you are going to keep drowning. Hope for what you can't see, and then believe.

• Have you lost hope?

• Do you wish you could hope?

> *This hope will not disappoint because the love of God has been poured out into our hearts.*
>
> Romans 5:5

NOTES

CHAPTER TEN

ENDURE

Endurance is one of the most critical steps to breathing underwater. The funny thing about endurance is that you can only gain endurance through trials. It's the old adage, "no pain, no gain." Like anything that matters in life, building endurance takes work. For those with tough situations, we have a great training program.

Last spring, I was leading the worship for a retreat on Long Island. On this retreat, my bedroom was as far from the main conference room as you could get. It was down a very long hallway and around the corner into another wing. Inevitably, I was running back and forth in a hurry between my room, the conference room and the chapel. Because I needed to open the sessions with music, and because I always forgot something I needed, I was literally running from one room to another. On Friday night, it started off as a dainty pace, in heels. By Saturday morning, I was wearing flip flops, but I still found it hard to get anywhere fast. By Saturday evening, I was barefoot and truly jogging down the hall.

That's when I heard that familiar voice speak to me, "I want you to start running." Smiling and nodding to the ladies as I flew past, I assured them that the retreat session was starting on time, I thought, "Lord, I am running like I always do, from one thing to the next." But then I became aware of how my body felt as I jogged down the hall. I noticed that my steps were sure and steady and the anxiety over all I needed to accomplish seemed to fade to the background as my body moved. For me, MS affects my balance on my right side, in particular when I am walking on stairs. When I close my eyes, I can't steady myself because I have lost some sensation in my right foot. But I noticed that as I jogged, it seemed to wake up my foot in way that walking doesn't. I wondered if there was something to this request, even while I reminded the Lord that *I don't run.*

Monday morning, I woke up with the birds and the puppy (don't ask), and for a fleeting moment, as I put on my sneakers for my morning walk, I thought about running. However, that familiar statement, "I don't run," was sabotaging any thought of trying. I put the puppy back in the crate for breakfast and set out for my walk, with adult dogs in tow and rosary in hand.

I love my early morning rosary walks. Contrary to some common mis-understandings, the rosary isn't focused on Mary, the mother of Jesus. It's a series of rote prayers, one for each bead, that are designed to lead a person to consider the mysteries of the life of Jesus. Each decade, or ten prayers, is a different mystery to contemplate. I work out my troubles in my daily rosary walk, talking with Jesus and his Mom.

This one morning as I started my brisk walk, I felt the desire to run welling up in me. I was also feeling some anxiety and I thought maybe I'd walk a little and then jog a little. Before I knew it, I was jogging off and on with each decade of the rosary. With each step, I felt more exhilarated and steady on my feet. Each day, I woke up and got excited to run. It helped me to focus my prayer and work out any anxiety that I was feeling.

It was a strange transformation that happened in me. I started doing a walk/run every day, eventually gearing up to do my first 5K. By the end of this year, I will have done three 5Ks in four months and logged countless miles and prayers on my rosary run/walk.

I have decided that despite my long held belief that I don't run, I do now. My sister-in-law, Carol, started a running group called Annie's Locker (annieslocker.org). Their runs are called "Running for Two." They were inspired by a friend who died of cancer, a woman named Annie, who used her runs as a prayerful and therapeutic tool for endurance. The group offers their runs and their prayers as intentions for those who struggle. Back in March, they sponsored a fundraising "Running for Two" for Johanna's Hope for a Cure. They collected donations for us to defray some of our medical expenses. Carol and her group inspire me to endure the run for Johanna and for my family who needs my prayers and my strength to continue the race.

As I run and pray, I am building endurance. I am building endurance and bodily strength to go the extra mile, not just in a 5K. When you struggle with autoimmune disease, like I do, endurance is a key to health. Building endurance in my body tells my body that it can handle the ups and downs of autoimmune issues. Exercise, gait and balance training help me to endure the neurological disconnect that often accompanies MS. It helps me to know that I have what it takes to keep going, no matter what happens.

Combining exercise with prayer builds my spiritual and mental endurance. It gives me an outlet and a focus to alleviate anxiety and stress in an appropriate way. It also ensures that I am taking care of myself first. Much like the oxygen mask on the airplane, if I can't breathe, I can't help my daughter or anyone else.

Endurance is defined as the ability or strength to continue or last, especially despite fatigue, stress or other adverse conditions. We all need endurance to keep going when life gets tough.

The Bible goes so far as to promise that our difficulties can actually produce endurance, which in turn strengthens our character and gives us hope.

> *And not only that, but we also rejoice in our afflictions, because we know that affliction produces endurance, endurance produces proven character, and proven character produces hope. This hope does not disappoint, because God's love has been poured out in our hearts through the Holy Spirit who was given to us.*
>
> Romans 5:3-5

I know this scripture is true. I have seen it happen in my life and the lives of many other people I know. Like that saying, "What doesn't kill you makes you stronger," endurance strengthens us to take the next step. When we take that step, despite the struggle, we become encouraged and hopeful that we can keep moving forward. On my morning prayer walk/run, I am also building endurance, for the race of my life, one bead and one step at time.

My husband and I have two symbols of endurance that we wear every day—our wedding bands. Steve's ring belonged to his grandfather and his dad. It's a large black onyx stone with a diamond chip in the middle. The diamond chip was from his grandmother's engagement ring, on his dad's side. When Steve's grandfather died, the ring was passed down to Steve's dad. Then, when Steve's dad died, the family heirloom was passed down to him. It was a little big for my husband, but rather than adding a ring adjuster, Steve had his wedding band fitted inside. The ring is over 50 years old.

About eight years ago, the diamond fell out of my engagement ring. I was thinking about getting it set back in when my mother gave me her wedding and engagement rings. She had lost the diamond many years ago and had never replaced it. My diamond was just the right size for her ring. So, we took it to the jeweler and had it all sized and fitted.

My mother's wedding and engagement rings were also her mother's rings. My grandparents' initials and the date of their wedding are engraved inside the wedding ring. My grandparents were married on November 24, 1919. My wedding and engagement rings are ninety–five years old.

Both my husband's ring and my rings—our wedding rings—are symbols which span over three generations of marriages. They are signs of enduring love. My husband and I, in our marriage, are signs of enduring love.

Falling in love is easy. Staying in love requires endurance, especially when that love is tried by extreme trials and raising a child who is medically fragile with special needs.

As I said in the beginning of the book, Johanna was our 10th anniversary gift to each other. She was and is God's gift to us for saying yes to His gift of life. Johanna has been with us for the greater part of our marriage. My husband always said from the beginning that situations like these make a good marriage stronger and a bad marriage worse. I used to put us in the former category. But if we are honest with one another, our marriage lands right in the middle.

Over the years, my husband and I worked very hard at finding time for each other amidst the flurry of hospitalizations and regular life. During very long hospitalizations we took time to leave the hospital and go out by ourselves.

As the years went on, balancing work, family and frequent hospitalizations got tougher. Even in church ministry, the best bosses lose patience when their employees constantly have to adjust their schedules for a family crisis. Community and family support also waned as time went on. There were over twenty people in the waiting room with us for Johanna's first brain surgery. By the time she had her sixth, in that very first year, Steve and I were the only ones in the waiting room. In the beginning, there were meals arranged for us when Johanna was in the hospital. As the months turned into years, the meals stopped and people just figured that we were used to this way of life. In truth, we were. But it didn't mean that we didn't need the support.

We learned strategies for coping, some good and some not so good. Caring for Johanna became my primary job and I was really good at it. Economic and social pressures weighed on my husband as it was obvious that his employer was tiring of the chronic nature of this disease. When Johanna was in a coma, one friend even asked if we were just postponing the inevitable, as if we had a choice. Disconnecting a six year old from life support was not even an option we'd considered. Questions like that came up frequently from people who cared but who did not want to see us continue to endure such pain.

The economic stresses over the last six years have put a considerable strain on our marriage. When my husband's church administrator position was eliminated, it felt like God fired him. Churches all over the country were downsizing just like corporate America. We got the message that it was time to move on from ministry and embrace new careers as entrepreneurs. It was exciting and scary, kind of like we were pioneers moving out in search of a new way of life.

 However, when you leave a career that is also connected to a foundation that you have based your life on, cracks appear where the pieces were broken off. Other weak areas also suddenly appear and you realize the whole foundation needs some repair. We are repairing those cracks and shoring up the foundation so that it can endure rebuilding. We rebuild because we believe that love endures.

There are some frightening statistics on the health of marriages and families who care for children with special needs, disabled adults and the elderly. The statistics show that caregivers and their families are drowning. It's easy for a caregiver to get discouraged.

What cannot be expressed in the statistics is the mystery that surpasses all understanding—*love endures.*

Every human being knows this truth; it is written in our DNA. Life persists in the face of extreme trials, defying all odds because of this one truth—*love endures.*

As the Mom of four beautiful children and the caregiver of one with special needs, I know how hard it is to endure. We think that endurance means getting away from the problems and even distancing ourselves from the person for whom we are caregiving. But in truth, it is they who help us to endure, because they call us to unconditional love.

This past summer I was able to visit with one of my older sisters who is afflicted by a neuro-degenerative disease. We grew up together. She is five years older than me. Five years ago, she was still walking, talking and driving on her own. Now she requires 24/7 care and is in a wheelchair. This summer I got to see her three times, which was such a blessing because we live far away.

It was really hard to see my big sister reduced to the cognitive and physical abilities of a young child. In many ways, she requires more functional care than my daughter, Johanna. In fact, Johanna rose to the occasion to help her aunt in a beautiful way. Johanna pushed my sister in the wheelchair and spent time with her playing simple games and reading books. It was a very special time.

I witnessed in my sister's family the same overwhelming issues that we have faced over the years. And I also witnessed the hope of enduring love. As roles reversed from child and spouse to parent and caregiver, a precious truth unfolded. My sister, much like my daughter, has a wisdom that is beyond her ability. Once in a while, she comes out with words that remind us of this mystery. Early on in our visit, my big sister gazed into my teary eyes and said, "I'm still here." In that moment enduring love touched the depths of my soul. I knew my sister's knowledge was outside the confines of this disease, revealing the wisdom of God.

Jesus put it this way:

> *I praise you, Father, Lord of heaven and earth, because you have hidden these things from the wise and learned, and revealed them to little children....And whoever welcomes one such child in my name welcomes me.*
>
> Matthew 11:25, 18:5

These little ones in our midst: the unborn, the children with special needs, the infirmed spouses, disabled adults and elderly parents; they are the ones who teach us to love and to endure because they are windows to heaven. We see life from a whole different perspective when we care for the little ones.

REFLECT

The key to enduring—and to breathing underwater—is to embrace our loved ones unconditionally and give them the respect and honor they deserve. As we welcome them, we welcome God into our lives and we touch eternity.

• Who are the little ones in your life who teach you to love so that you may endure?

• Welcome them and embrace them today.

Love bears all things, believes all things, hopes all things and endures all things. Love never fails.
1 Corinthians 13:7

NOTES

A FINAL JOURNEY OF HOPE

Since I turned 21, I have spent most of my birthdays on a day of prayer by myself. When the kids were young, I took a few hours away from home at a retreat house or a church. But when they got older, as long as Johanna was stable, I went for an overnight retreat.

It's my yearly visit with just me and God, to recap the year and get a glimpse for the future. Because my birthday is the week before Christmas, it is also a nice Advent day of prayer. Last year was a big birthday. I turned 50. I made reservations at the retreat house, but at the last minute the nuns needed to cancel. 2013 was a very hard year for Johanna and for me. I needed this badly. So, I made a reservation at a nearby hotel and created my own retreat.

It started with dinner with two very dear friends. There was plenty of laughter and some tears. Then I headed back to the hotel, just down the street from the restaurant. I blocked the door with a chair because I really don't like staying alone, even though I like being alone. Then I settled in for a wonderful sleep. I got up early the next morning and ran to daily Mass, which truly is the highlight of my day. I had breakfast at the hotel and then raced back upstairs to spend my morning writing and praying.

That morning reflection changed my perspective on many things. Instead of being a time to review the year (did I mention how hard it was?), the Lord helped me to connect the dots of the past 50 years. Truly, it was a lifetime in review, and it was very cool indeed.

I saw my life at 50 as a convergence of visions, hopes and dreams that were finally coming together. I wrote the convergence in my journal, and I knew that this was the year it would all make sense. I realized then that the year ahead would be a year of fulfillment, where things that I have pondered since childhood would finally make sense and in some ways, come to pass.

Writing this book is the expression of this convergence. In the preface, I shared with you a vision I had as a teenager. The vision of the little rose that was placed in my hands and lifted up to reveal streams of light in every direction came with a promise: "This little rose shall become a light to the nations."

Johanna's middle name is Rose, after St. Therese, The Little Flower. St. Therese never traveled the world; she lived a very ordinary life and through it she became an extraordinary saint. Her life's message is known the world over as "The Little Way of Love." It has been embraced by all who seek to live a holy life in our everyday world.

I now realize Johanna is the Rose in my hands that was promised in my youth. Along with my other three children, she has taught me to love and be courageous in ways that I never thought possible. Johanna in particular has been a light to nations. People we don't even know are touched by her life, her strength, her humor and by her humble way to simply love.

Johanna points us all towards heaven. Sometimes more than we'd like, she reminds us that life on earth is not our true home, that we are destined for heaven. At the beginning of 2013, in the midst of a very difficult hospital stay, Johanna opened a portal for me, a window to this world we call our heavenly home.

It was the middle of the night and she woke up groaning. When I got up to look at her, she was staring straight ahead. I called her name and touched her arm but she didn't respond. She just stared. I called the nurse; she checked all the monitors. Johanna's numbers were stable, but she still just stared and we suspected it was a seizure. Her pupils were very sluggish and she did not respond to our call. Then finally, as if a switch turned on or off, she turned her gaze to me without any medical intervention. The nurse left and put a note in the chart that suggested a seizure. I climbed into bed with Johanna because I was really afraid that she would just slip away.

Then all of sudden Johanna started speaking, and words bubbled out from her like a waterfall. She told me that our home is really close. When I said Jamesport is kind of far from New York City, she shook her head and said that Jesus took her to heaven and it's really very close. That's when I grabbed my iPhone to take notes as she continued:

> *Jesus took me to heaven on an elephant.*
> *Mama, our real home is really close;*
> *Heaven is just a hop, skip and a jump away.*
>
> *It's very close, Mama; it's very close.*
> *Jesus showed me heaven and He told me that heaven is my home.*
> *He told me, "Someday this will be your forever home."*
> *It's royal blue. Mary is at His side. Me on His lap.*
> *It's really close now; a hop, a skip and a jump away.*
>
> *He told me to trust Him.*
> *I said, "I do. Every day I put my trust in You."*
>
> *Jesus took me there on an elephant. I saw a rainbow.*

I asked Johanna what heaven felt like and she said,

It felt offering, offering, offering;
My offering to heaven and heaven's offering to me.

They opened the gate of heaven for me and Jesus.
There was a chair for me and a chair for Jesus.
There was two crowns: one for me and one for Jesus.
And two chalices filled with wine: one for me and one for Jesus.

After we ate and drank and then Jesus said to me,
"Your time has come. Get up and walk with me as your Master.
I will never leave you. I wish you could stay with me right now but
unfortunately your earthly pilgrimage has not yet come to an end."

After that night, there were no more staring episodes, and the EEG they ran to test for seizures was completely normal. Johanna doesn't remember that night or the details of that dream, but when I share the notes I took while she was talking, she smiles and nods. It all comes back to her in pictures.

She did for me, and for all of us, what she has been doing since the moment of her conception in my womb. Johanna revealed that this life is a journey of hope leading us to Heaven.

It's really close now; Heaven is only a hop, a skip and a jump away.

ABOUT THE AUTHOR

Eileen Benthal is a writer, speaker and certified professional coach who specializes in coaching caregivers. She is a graduate of Franciscan University with a degree in Theology and a minor in English. She combines her academic education, years of ministry to women and life-changing experiences as a caregiver for her medically fragile child to offer hope to the hopeless. One of her stories about her daughter was published in a treasured collection of essays entitled: *A Special Mother is Born*. She has also co-authored the journal *Navigating Deep Waters: Meditations for Caregivers*.

Eileen has been published in local and national publications including *The Word Among Us*. Her family's story about their commitment to Canine Companions for Independence was also featured in The New York Times. Eileen writes a weekly column entitled "Life on Purpose," which is published in RiverheadLocal.com and SoutholdLocal.com, and she contributes a bi-weekly community column for Times/Review Publications.

Eileen is a fierce defender for the dignity of all human life and a speaker who advocates for families and people with disabilities. She has spoken at a press conference on healthcare at the Capitol in DC, on the nationally syndicated Sean Hannity radio show, *Hannity* and *Fox & Friends* on Fox News, as well as Relevant Radio's *Drew Mariani Show*. Her interviews were also replayed on Rush Limbaugh's radio program.

A gifted motivational speaker, Eileen speaks from her heart and inspires from a place of faith in God to help those who seek strength and purpose in the midst of grave trials.

Eileen has been married to her husband Steve for over twenty-five years and is the mother of four young adult children. They live on the North Fork of Long Island with their service dogs where they enjoy spectacular views of vineyards, the water and the sky.

To place orders and find current information on upcoming book signings and events, visit www.BreathingUnderwater.info.

Reviews, endorsements, articles and photographs of the stories told in this book can be found on www.BreathingUnderwater.com and/or www.CareforaCaregiver.com.

Follow us on Facebook:
Facebook.com/BreathingUnderwaterCaregiversJourneyofHope
Facebook.com/CareforaCaregiver

SPEAKING ENGAGEMENTS

Eileen is a very gifted motivational speaker who shares from her heart to touch a wide array of audiences. She is an experienced keynote speaker and panelist for large conferences and workshops, as well as an inspiring retreat presenter for large and small groups.

Using storytelling and multimedia presentations, Eileen shares inspirational and practical solutions for dealing with chronic and emergent situations. She highlights topics appropriate to caregivers and others who are struggling with economic loss, health challenges or personal loss.

Eileen presents Breathing Underwater to professional and family

caregivers, church and civic support groups alike. Diverse groups and individuals relate to the feelings and frustrations of being overwhelmed by life. While Breathing Underwater easily addresses the needs of family caregivers, it is well suited for anyone who feels that they are overwhelmed and drowning in their circumstances.

Using the acronym BREATHE, Eileen highlights strategies to help others learn to breathe when they feel like they are drowning.

Each event is geared to the specific target audiences, while the basic message remains the same. The large and small group process is where the emphasis of the presentations is tailored to meets the needs of the group.

In addition to speaking at conferences, retreats and workshops, Eileen is a certified professional coach who offers group and one to one coaching for caregivers or people who struggle with life threatening and/or chronic health issues.

Visit www.CareforaCaregiver.com and www.BreathingUnderwater.info for more information. For writing, speaking and coaching, contact Eileen directly at eileenbenthal@gmail.com.

RESOURCES

Here are some helpful websites for more support.

ADVOCACY

Canine Companions for Independence
An wonderful organization providing assistance dogs to people with disabilities. Our family has been greatly enhanced by CCI. www.CCI.org

Angioma Alliance
The Angioma Alliance is a grass roots organization that supports research and families like ours who are affected by cavernous angiomas. www.AngiomaAlliance.org

National Organization for Rare Disorders
A clearing house of resources for those lives afflicted with rare diseases. www.RareDiseases.org

Today's Caregiver
This organization provides excellent free resources for caregivers in their online newsletter and Fearless Caregiver Regional Conferences. www.Caregiver.com

HEALTH

Amen Clinics
These clinics assess the brain through SPECT scan imaging. They focus on living a healthy lifestyle to heal your brain and change your life. www.AmenClinics.com

Dr. Mark Hyman
One of my favorite doctors for support on healing the body with good nutrition. www.DrHyman.com

SPIRITUAL SUPPORT

The Word Among Us
This is an online and print Scripture and meditation resource that I have used every day for the past 30 years. www.WAU.org

Magnificat: A Ministry to Catholic Women
This is a wonderful outreach for dynamic faith support for Catholic women. There are chapters all over the world.
www.Magnificat-Ministry.net

Unbound
This is an ecumenical ministry to those who need prayer for inner healing and deliverance from evil with resources around the world.
www.HeartoftheFather.com

ENTREPRENEURIAL SUPPORT

Caregivers need opportunities to earn income from home. Check out these links and contact me to help you decide if they are right for you.

Isagenix International
Isagenix products are a tremendous foundation for health. Direct sales companies are an excellent way to start a home business. Explore the possibility of working with me to improve your health and achieve financial stability while working from home.
www.FreeIndeed.Isagenix.com

International Coach Certification Academy
See if you've got what it takes to make a living while you make a difference as a professional coach. Take Drs. Glenn and Sharon Livingston's FREE Coaching Test and discover your personal strengths and weaknesses in the coaching industry in a FREE custom report.
www.TheCoachingTest.com

44190966R00084

Made in the USA
Charleston, SC
17 July 2015